Bicycling Magazine's

Basic Maintenance and Repair

By the Editors of *Bicycling* Magazine

Rodale Press, Emmaus, Pennsylvania

Copyright © 1990 by Rodale Press, Inc.

Printed in the United States of America on acid-free paper and recycled paper (∞)

Compiled and edited by *Ed Pavelka*

Production editor: *Jane Sherman*
Copy editor: *Durrae Johanek*
Cover and interior design: *Lisa Farkas*
Cover photo: *T. L. Gettings*

If you have any questions or comments concerning this book, please write:
  Rodale Press
  Book Reader Service
  33 East Minor Street
  Emmaus, PA 18098

Library of Congress Cataloging-in-Publication Data

Bicycling magazine's basic maintenance and repair / by the editors of
  Bicycling magazine.
      p.   cm.
  ISBN 0-87857-902-8   paperback
  1. Bicycles—Maintenance and repair.   I. Bicycling.   II. Title: Basic
maintenance and repair.
  TL430.B54   1990
  629.28'772—dc20   89-70255
                                                                  CIP

Distributed in the book trade by St. Martin's Press

  4 6 8 10 9 7 5   paperback

CONTENTS

Introduction v

Part One: Basic Maintenance
   1 Home Shop Tools 1
   2 Weekly Maintenance 5
   3 Lightning Lube 8
   4 Eliminating Ticks and Rattles 9
   5 Wash and Wax 14

Part Two: Tires and Wheels
   6 Clincher Tire Repair 18
   7 Pump Repair 21
   8 Wheel Truing 24
   9 Spoke Replacement 28
  10 Easy Rim Replacement 31

Part Three: Brakes
  11 Servicing Caliper Brakes 37
  12 Cantilevers and U-Brakes 40

Part Four: Gear System
  13 Installing and Adjusting an Index Shifting
      System 47
  14 Gear System Tune-Up 52
  15 Chain Care 57
  16 Freewheel Cog Replacement 60

Part Five: Internal Bearings
   17 Crankset Overhaul 65
   18 Hub Overhaul 70
   19 Headset Overhaul 74
   20 Pedal Overhaul 78
Part Six: Mountain Bike Maintenance
   21 Care and Cleaning 81
Part Seven: Detailing
   22 Frame Paint Touch-Up 88
   23 Weatherproofing 91
   24 Personal Adjustments 94
Part Eight: Special Occasions
   25 Spring Tune-Up 102
   26 Emergency Repair Kit 106
   27 Post-Crash Inspection 110
   28 Breaking in a New Bike 114
   29 Pre-Event Checklist 116
Credits 120

 Introduction

Perhaps the most intriguing aspect of cycling is how the rider and machine combine to expand the limits of human-powered performance. Your bicycle becomes an extension of your body, moving you with a grace and efficiency unmatched by other forms of transportation.

And yet a bicycle is so simple. Most parts are in plain view, able to be watched and touched. When you see them become dirty or damaged, when they begin malfunctioning due to lack of lubrication, improper adjustment, or wear, they're easy to service. This book will tell you how. Read each procedure carefully, work slowly, and we guarantee that you'll be able to keep your bike in top shape. The benefits are obvious, but there's also this bonus: When you understand how each part of your bike works, you'll ride with much more confidence and enthusiasm.

This book contains a solution to almost every mechanical problem. Some repairs require replacement parts and special tools that can be purchased from professional bicycle dealers. We recommend buying the best-quality tools you can. They'll last a lifetime and help you work with an expert's touch.

All procedures are the same as those presented in *Bicycling* magazine's "Repair Stand" column by two editors, Don Cuerdon and Jim Langley, who are former pro bike mechanics. For an even more detailed explanation of bike repair, including scores of photographs, we refer you to *Bicycling Magazine's Complete Guide to Maintenance and Repair,* published by Rodale Press.

Ed Pavelka, Executive Editor
Bicycling Magazine

Part One

BASIC
MAINTENANCE

∎1 HOME SHOP TOOLS

This book will describe many maintenance and repair procedures that can be performed even by newcomers to cycling. There's only one catch: To do the work, you need certain general and specialized tools. You don't need to duplicate the collection found on the tool board at a bike shop—that would cost thousands of dollars—but let's see which tools you should own and which are better left to the pros.

Work Stand

A good work stand is essential. Turning the bike upside down just won't do. The brake cables deform, it's hard to see the derailleur adjusting screws, and it's disorienting.

The simplest stand is made by Persons and costs about $8. You may see them used for bike displays in the local shop window. Other stands generally cost between $30 and $100, depending on their features. Some fold for easy storage, a good idea for apartment dwellers with limited space.

Look for a stand that allows the front wheel to remain on the bike, as opposed to one that holds the fork by the dropouts. The latter prohibits adjustments to the front brake and headset.

Basic Tools

The following tools can be bought in most hardware stores. If you need to economize, do it on wrenches, not screwdrivers. Most bicycle nuts and bolts will deform or break long before the cheapest wrench shows any strain. Cheap screwdrivers, on the other hand, dull easily and mangle hard-to-replace items such as derailleur adjustment screws.

Wrenches. Most bikes have metric nuts and bolts. Start with a set of box or open-end wrenches sized from 8 to 17 mm in 1mm increments. Expect to spend $10 to $15. (Those of you still riding vintage Raleighs and 1958 Schwinn Jaguars will have to buy Whitworth and American wrenches in addition to the metric set.)

Also buy 12- and 6-inch adjustable wrenches. The former is for applying force to a freewheel remover and the headset locknut. The latter is for toeing in brake calipers and front derailleur cages. Together they can be used for straightening chainrings and crank spiders. Neither wrench should be used for turning nuts or bolts (with the exception of the headset), because they're likely to slip and round the corners. Decent adjustable wrenches can be bought for $5 to $15, depending on size.

Next, buy hex wrenches (also called Allen keys) for working on the stem, seatpost, bottle cage bolts, and the like. Don't get a set, because you'll have more oddball sizes than useful ones. These sizes should suffice: 2 through 7mm, 1/8-, 3/16-, 1/4-inch. Hex wrenches cost $1 or less.

Screwdrivers. Again, there's no need to buy an entire set for bike maintenance. You'll need standard screwdrivers with blade widths of 1/4 and 1/8 inch, and Phillips screwdrivers with small and medium heads. Quality screwdrivers cost about $5 each.

Pliers. Three types are useful. Locking pliers, such as those made by Vise-Grip, are handy for grabbing bolts rounded by adjustable wrenches. The 6-inch size costs $5 to $7. Channellock-type pliers can do almost everything that slip-joint and long-nose pliers can, and they're handy for squeezing flares out of rims. An 8-inch pair costs $6 to $10. Diagonal cutters are handy for trimming cables, housing, toe straps, and handlebar tape. Figure on spending $5 to $7 for a 6-inch pair.

Mallet. A 1-pound wooden or rubber mallet is the best tool for loosening a handlebar expander bolt, driving a pin punch, or removing a rim dent. Don't use a steel hammer or you'll damage the bike. Do use a block of wood if your budget can't afford a mallet.

Photograph 1-1. Bike maintenance tools include, at top from left to right, wrenches, a screwdriver, pliers, a mallet, crankarm tools, and bottom bracket tools. At bottom, from left to right, are freewheel removers, spoke wrenches, tire levers, a third-hand tool, a chain rivet extractor, a headset wrench, and cone wrenches.

Specialty Tools

You'll need several bicycle-specific tools found only in shops and catalogs. Some tools are made for particular brands of components, while others are more universal. If you become proficient working on your bike, it's likely the word will spread, and you'll occasionally be fixing others. Therefore, it's better to buy the universal tool when there is the option.

Crankarm tools. Two tools are necessary to remove cotterless crankarms, one to unscrew the fixing bolts and the other to pull the arms off the crank axle. Bolt wrenches cost $3 to $7 and come in 14, 15, and 16 mm. The Park universal wrench with all three sizes sells for $10 to $12. If you own a socket driver, you may be able to get at the bolts with a thin-wall socket.

Park also makes a universal extractor that services virtually all cranks and costs $12 to $15. Otherwise, an extractor must be purchased for each brand at $5 to $8 per tool.

Bottom bracket tools. Nearly all bottom brackets can be serviced with two tools (in addition to the crankarm tools). Lockring pliers have a slip joint for accommodating any size lockring. They cost about $10 per pair. Add another $4 to $6 for a universal pin tool to fit the adjustable cup. Generally, inexpensive fixed cup tools don't work well, and the professional tool is expensive. So when fixed cup replacement becomes necessary, visit a pro mechanic.

If you want to work on a bike with a sealed bottom bracket cartridge, you may have to buy tools made for the unit. Inquire at a bike shop.

Freewheel remover. There are no universal tools in this department. Every freewheel manufacturer makes a remover with unique dimensions. The freewheel must be removed for servicing the rear hub and replacing spokes. Buy one remover for each brand of freewheel you plan to encounter. The price ranges from $2.50 to $7.00.

For those of you with cassette freehubs instead of freewheels, invest in a pair of chainwhips ($10 to $15 per pair) for removing the cogs.

Spoke wrench. There are three common spoke nipple sizes: Japanese, French, and DT. Park makes very good spoke wrenches in each size for around $4 each, but not a universal tool. For occasional truing (as opposed to wheelbuilding) a $2 universal tool works fine.

Tire levers. There's nothing better than tire levers for removing clincher tires. A set of three in plastic, steel, or alloy won't exceed $3.

Third-hand tool. This $2-to-$4 tool holds the brake pads against the rim to free your hands for the cable adjustment.

Chain rivet extractor. A derailleur-equipped bike doesn't have a master link in the chain, so a rivet extractor is necessary for chain removal and installation. The Cyclo Rivoli is a good choice for about $6.

Headset wrench. To adjust most headsets you need a flat 32mm wrench for turning the upper race nut. Park has one with a 15mm pedal wrench at the opposite end for about $8. Certain headsets, such as Mavic and Shimano 600, require special tools.

Cone wrenches. These special flat wrenches allow you to adjust and overhaul hubs. The 13mm size doubles as a caliper centering tool in many brakesets. Buy two cone wrenches in the 13–14mm size and two in the 15–16mm size. Pay extra to get Campagnolo, Park, or Bicycle Research, because cheap cone wrenches don't last. Use the 17mm wrench from the box or open-end set for the occasional French locknut.

Floor pump with gauge. Underinflated tires perform poorly, wear quickly, and contribute to rim damage. A high-pressure pump with a built-in gauge eliminates guesswork. Prices range from $20 to $35.

2 WEEKLY MAINTENANCE

During much of the year you probably ride several times a week. To keep your bike working efficiently and reliably, devote some time each week to cleaning, lubricating, and adjusting. This general maintenance will also help you find a problem before it results in a breakdown. If a repair is necessary, consult the appropriate chapter for instructions.

Clean and Inspect

Put your bike in a work stand or against a support. Unless the frame is filthy, use a soft rag to polish it with a cleaner/wax such as Bike Elixir. Otherwise, wash it with a brush and mild detergent, then rinse and dry it well.

As you clean, inspect for frame damage. Look for bulges and cracks in the metal, especially at tube intersections. If you find any, have the problem evaluated by a pro mechanic. Use touch-up paint on scratches or chips that expose bare metal.

Next, dip a corner of your rag in a solvent such as kerosene, or spray it with a lubricant such as WD-40 or Tri-Flow. Wipe each component clean, inspecting for cracks, loose bolts, and so on as you work. Save the drivetrain (crankset and derailleurs) for last because these parts are usually the dirtiest.

Do not clean rims with solvent, which can leave an oily film that renders the brakes useless. Instead, wipe the rims with a clean, dry rag. Inspect each spoke hole for cracks and for ferrules pulling through. Look for dents or gouges in the sidewalls. Replace a damaged rim immediately.

Wipe the spokes and squeeze each pair to find any that are loose or broken. Spin each wheel and watch the rim where it passes the brake pads. If you see large wobbles or hops, true the wheel before riding again or the rim could become damaged beyond repair. Check for loose hub bearings by wiggling the rim side to side. There should be no play.

Examine each tire's tread for embedded glass or other debris. Potential puncture producers can often be removed before they work through the tire casing. Also check the tread and sidewalls for cuts and bulges. Damaged tires *must* be replaced immediately. Their failure is inevitable. If you have tubular tires, try to push them off the rim with your thumbs. If they budge, reglue them.

Squeeze and Wiggle

Firmly squeeze each brake lever. Anything pop loose? Make sure each pad contacts the rim properly and recedes about 2 mm when the lever is released. Make fine cable adjustments with the barrels on the calipers or brake levers.

Check the headset adjustment by squeezing the front brake lever and rocking the bike back and forth. Clunking indicates looseness. If it sounds okay, lift the front wheel slightly and nudge the handlebar. Does the headset seem to catch when the wheel points straight ahead? A worn or tight headset reduces steering control, so have it repaired soon. Place an ear against the tip of the saddle and turn the handlebar. Rumbling means the bearings are dry or dirty.

Grasp a crankarm and wiggle it side to side. There shouldn't be play. A loose crankset will impair shifting and wear out prematurely. Tap each chainring bolt. If one is loose, you'll hear it. Once a month, remove the pedals, unship the chain, and check the condition of the bottom bracket bearings by putting your ear to the saddle as you turn the crank.

While the pedals are off, turn their axles and feel for roughness. Inspect the toe clips for cracks and loose bolts. Check the straps for wear and damaged buckles.

Grasp the saddle by the tip and tail, and shake it in all directions. Do the same with the handlebar. Tighten anything that slips. Check the nuts and bolts on accessories such as bottle cages and racks. Make sure there's a fresh spare tube or tire in your tool kit, and be certain your frame pump works.

Lube and Inflate

The two surest (and simplest) ways to help your bike work well are to maintain proper tire pressure and frequently lubricate your chain. A lubed chain shifts better, runs quieter, and lasts longer. Full tires roll efficiently and protect your rims from damage.

Chain maintenance is a simple matter of wiping the links clean with a rag, then applying a lubricant. This can be done with the chain on the bike. If the chain is filled with sludge, however, you'll need to remove it and use a solvent.

Recommended tire pressure is usually printed on the sidewall. In general, high-pressure clinchers and training tubulars require about 110 psi. If you're in doubt, call a bike shop. Most floor pumps with a built-in gauge are reasonably accurate. The pumps at gas stations are risky to use because they quickly deliver a large volume of air, which can blow out a bike tire.

Once you've established your weekly maintenance routine, the work will take only about 20 minutes. This small amount of time pays off big in confidence, safety, and smooth, efficient riding.

■3■ LIGHTNING LUBE

It never fails. You're dressed and ready to leave. Anxious to start riding, you do a quick preride check—squeezing brake levers ("squeak, squeak"), turning cranks and checking the drivetrain ("chirp, chirp"), tugging on the handlebar ("cre-e-e-ak"). Unless you're the type who likes to attract attention by scraping your fingernails down a chalkboard, these squeaks, chirps, and creaks will eventually drive you and your training partners crazy. You need a quick solution.

Instead of slamming ol' wonderhorse back in the garage, grab a can of your favorite liquid lubricant and spend 5 minutes evicting the crickets and birdies. Aerosol spray is okay, but apply it through a thin plastic tube so it doesn't splatter. Just in case, keep a rag handy for wiping drips.

Creaking from the bottom bracket, pedal axles, or hubs indicates more serious problems that should be cured with an overhaul.

Drivetrain

1. Put your bike in the repair stand, or lean it against a wall with the derailleur side facing you.

2. While slowly turning the crank backward with your right hand, apply a small amount of lubricant to each chain link as it passes over the freewheel.

3. Let the oil soak into the chain while you lube the rest of the bike. When you're done, wipe away the excess with a lint-free rag.

4. Apply a bit more lubricant to the edge of the plate on either side of each rear derailleur pulley (near the top so it can ooze down). Wipe away the excess.

5. Bottom bracket cable guides also need to be lubed. You may have to tip the bike up on the rear wheel to access under-bottom bracket guides. Also lube the points where cables enter or exit cable stops or housing. Again, wipe away the excess.

Brakes

1. Squeeze each brake lever handle, then lube the cable end button and each side of the handle where it hinges inside the housing.

2. Lube the caliper arms where they meet at the pivot bolt. Lube the spot on each arm that contacts the spring, being careful not to overspray onto the pads or rim. Wipe away the excess.

Pedals and Shoes

1. Wet the corner of a paper towel with lubricant. Wipe both sides of the cage plate where the cleat contacts the pedal (or the cleat contact points of clipless pedals).

2. While the paper towel is still damp, rub it along the underside (the part that contacts your shoe) of each toe strap.

3. Apply some more lube between each cleat and shoe. Wipe away the excess (so you don't slip on the porch steps).

Handlebar and Saddle

1. Lean the bike over and lube where the handlebar enters the stem. Lean the bike the other way and lube this side, too. Wipe away the excess.

2. Wet the corner of a paper towel with lube and smear some on the underside of your saddle where it contacts the rails.

Okay, now the small choir will be silent, and your bike will work better to boot. So go ride in peace—and quiet.

4 ELIMINATING TICKS AND RATTLES

There's nothing more annoying than the mysterious noises that can haunt even a well-maintained bicycle. We've just seen how lubrication can eliminate squeaks and chirps, but what about those frustrating ticks, clicks, and rattles?

Crank/Pedal Ticks

This is a metallic click or snap during *every* crank revolution. You may even be able to feel it through your foot.

1. Check for loose connections. Unscrew each pedal, grease its threads, and tighten firmly to the crankarm. You may need to use a thin-jaw pedal wrench (remember the left pedal has backward threads; turn counterclockwise to install). Next, tighten each crankarm to the bottom bracket axle. You may have to remove a dustcap with an Allen key or screwdriver to gain access to the bolt.

2. Check for loose bottom bracket cups. If the crankarms have lateral play even though they are tight on the crank axle, the cups are not properly adjusted. Make the correction if you have the necessary tools; otherwise, take your bike to a pro mechanic.

3. Check for dry and/or worn ball bearings and races in the pedals and bottom bracket. Bearings become oval with wear. They may tick after their orientation is changed during repacking, so install new bearings every time you overhaul a part. Also check the bearing races for uneven wear, and replace them as necessary.

4. Check the front derailleur. Spray it with a penetrating lubricant such as Tri-Flow and make sure it's snugly attached to the seat tube. A dry or loose front derailleur on a flexible frame can cause a tick.

5. Check the pedal frames. A click is from a pedal rather than the chain if it occurs at the same place on each pedal stroke. Sometimes movement between the pedal's frame and its body causes this noise. Using the flex tube that comes with penetrants such as Tri-Flow or WD-40, spray each body/frame junction. Do the same where the toe clips attach, after making sure the bolts are tight.

Chain Clicks

A consistent click or jump in the drivetrain that doesn't

occur in sequence with the pedal stroke usually means a stiff chain link. Here's how to find and fix it.

1. Kneel on the right side of the bike and turn the crankarm backward. Carefully watch where the chain winds around the freewheel and through the derailleur pulleys. An unbending link will be apparent.

2. Grasp the chain on either side of the stiff link (use rags to keep your hands clean), and bend it laterally to loosen it.

3. Lubricate the formerly tight link with a product made for chains, and make sure to keep the entire chain properly maintained using the guidelines in chapter 15. Tight links are more likely to occur when a chain becomes dry or rusty.

Handlebar Creaks

This snapping and creaking usually occurs when you're sprinting or climbing, pulling hard on the handlebar.

1. Check the handlebar/stem junction. Make sure the

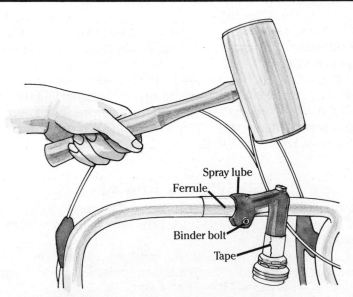

Illustration 1-1. Banishing handlebar creaks.

binder bolt is tight. If the noise persists, loosen the bolt and spray a penetrant between the bar and stem. Occasionally, the noise comes from a loose handlebar ferrule (the large-diameter center section). Have a professional mechanic inspect the bar if you suspect this is the problem.

2. Check the stem/steerer tube junction. Mark the stem height with a piece of tape. If you have aero brake levers, remove the front brake from the fork but leave the cable attached. Unscrew the stem's expander bolt four turns, then rap it sharply with a rubber or wooden mallet to free the plug. (See illustration 1-1.) Pull the stem from the steerer tube, grease it, reinsert it to the tape, and tighten the expander bolt after you align the stem with the front wheel.

Buzzing

Mysterious buzzing could mean your bike has one of these problems.

1. The water bottle is vibrating in its cage. For a metal cage, carefully bend it inward to hold the bottle tighter. For a plastic cage, wrap electrical tape around contact points with the bottle to snug the fit.

2. The brake cable housing is vibrating against the handlebar, stem, frame, or other housing. While riding, touch different sections of housing to locate the buzzing. By shortening, rerouting, or taping the housing you can eliminate the noise.

3. The pump has loose parts or is vibrating against the frame. Check the pump for tightness. If everything's in order, reposition it on the pump peg. Still buzzing? Wrap tape around the pump or frame where there's contact.

Rattles and Jingles

These can be tough to find, but here are four common culprits.

1. Tool bag. A loose under-saddle tool bag can bang against the seatpost, so secure it firmly. Inside, wrap loose, jingly tools with rubber bands or a rag.

2. Coins. Loose change in a jersey pocket can drive your riding partners batty. Try using a change purse, or put the coins in a plastic bag wrapped by a rubber band.

3. Lockrings. This classic mystery jingle occurs when the bottom bracket lockring loosens and rides on the axle. Immediate attention is required, or this dainty noise will be followed by the sound of bearings and races being pulverized. Tinkling is also heard when dustcaps loosen and bounce on the hub axles. Push them back into place with your thumbs.

4. Loose fittings. Anything that's attached to the frame—pump, computer, water bottle cage, racks, fenders—can rattle or vibrate loose. Regularly check all fittings, and use tape to deaden noise from metal-to-metal contact.

Thumping

This is usually felt rather than heard, and it occurs whether you're pedaling or coasting. Wheels are often the cause.

1. Check for dented rims. Spin each wheel and observe the rim where it passes the brake pads. Out-of-round rims can be trued; dented rims usually must be replaced.

2. Check for rim blips. These bulges in the sidewall cause thumping during braking. They result from hitting an object, such as the edge of a pothole, on underinflated tires. Blips can be carefully squeezed with Channellock-type pliers. You'll often create indents, which are the lesser of two evils. If your wheel thumps badly as the seam in the rim passes through the brake pads, take it to a pro mechanic for an evaluation.

3. Check for bulging tires. A tubular tire with a damaged casing looks like a snake after a good meal. A blowout is inevitable, so replace the tire. If this problem develops during a ride and you have no spare, reduce air pressure and be careful.

A clincher can bulge if the casing is damaged or the bead is improperly seated. Inspect the sidewall and tread for lumps, bulges, or tears. If there are none, spin the wheel and watch the bead line (it appears just above the rim). Slight fluctuations are normal, but if the line dips out of sight or hops significantly, deflate the tube and massage the tire at the trouble spots. Push the valve stem into the tire, then pull it down to make sure the tube isn't trapped under the edge.

5 WASH AND WAX

Sure, a clean bike looks nice, but it's also easier to work on, smoother to ride, and will last longer. Cleaning can also reveal faulty parts or frame defects before they become troublesome. With this in mind, pro team mechanics clean their riders' bikes after each day of racing.

You don't need to wash your bike after every ride. You can usually spruce it up with just a moist rag and some polish. But several times a year, particularly after off-road or foul-weather rides, you should wash it thoroughly.

Equipment

Cleaning a bike is a lot like cleaning a car. You'll need a hose, two buckets, sponges, rags, and stiff-bristle brushes of various sizes. (The Park Tool Company makes brushes designed for cleaning bicycles.) They should be marked with colored tape so you can keep those used on greasy parts separate from those used on the rest of the bike. This way you won't mistakenly smudge grease on your handlebar tape or saddle.

A bike stand is also useful. Don't turn the bike upside down for cleaning, as this will cause fluids to run into the headset and wash away grease.

In addition, you'll need a degreaser, diesel fuel, and soap. The Bike Elixir company makes a good liquid cleanser and a great paste wax for polishing the frame and components. It also makes Dave Moulton Frame Wax, designed for Du Pont Imron paint. This wax is less likely to accumulate in the nooks and crannies of a frame. In general, waxing isn't essential, but it does make subsequent cleanings easier.

Diesel fuel is good for cleansing drivetrain parts because it contains a small amount of oil. This ensures that parts will never be totally without lubrication. Simichrome, available at many bike shops and auto parts stores, is an abrasive paste that restores the luster of aluminum alloy.

It's possible to clean the chain with it on the bike. Park and Vetta both make good chain-cleaning devices that don't require removal. However, if the chain is covered with grime, remove it and soak it in diesel fuel. For this you'll need a chain rivet remover, a pan for soaking, and Tri-Flow or similar chain lubricant.

Use medium steel wool to remove surface frame rust. Deep rust or pitting can lead to structural failure, so have a mechanic examine such damage.

Do not use a product such as Armor-All on bike tires because it will make them slippery.

Cleaning

1. Put the bike on the repair stand and remove the wheels. If you plan to clean the chain without removing it, put a long screwdriver through the triangular holes in the rear dropouts and let the chain rest on it. This way you can turn the crank without having the chain scrape the right stay. Otherwise, remove the chain and put it in a pan of diesel fuel.

2. Fill two buckets with water. Put soap in one and soap and a small amount of diesel in the other. The bucket with soap is for cleaning the bike. The other is for drivetrain parts.

3. If you're cleaning the chain while it's on the bike, spray degreaser on it and the derailleurs, chainrings, and freewheel cogs. Don't use too much, and let it soak in.

In general, don't spray degreaser or water directly at the hubs, headset, freewheel body, pedals, or bottom bracket. Doing so will wash away grease from the bearings and cause wear. Always squirt from above rather than from the side.

4. While turning the crank, use a stiff brush dipped in diesel/soap mixture to scrub the top and bottom of the chain as it passes over the screwdriver. It might take several revolutions of the chain to get it clean. Continue pedaling and scrubbing, periodically dipping the brush in the mixture.

5. Brush the derailleurs and chainrings with the mixture until they're clean.

6. Use the soap solution and the other brushes and sponges to clean the rest of the bike. A sponge works best on handlebar tape, cables, and tubing. The brushes are for hard-to-reach spots. Never wipe off dirt or dried mud with a dry rag or brush because this will scratch the paint.

7. Rest the rear wheel on the bucket of diesel/soap

mixture and brush the freewheel cogs. Freewheel bodies have two sets of bearings: one under the smallest cog, the other under the largest. Avoid getting the fuel mixture in these areas.

8. Clean both wheels over the soap bucket. Use the sponges and brushes on the tires, rims, spokes, and hubs.

9. Hold the hose over the top of the bike and let a soft stream of water flow over the parts and frame. Do the same to the wheels.

10. Dry the bike with soft rags. Use separate rags for the drivetrain and frame.

11. Clean rubber deposits from the sidewalls of both rims. Acetone works well for this, but don't inhale it or let it touch your skin. Wear gloves and work in a well-ventilated area.

12. Wax the painted and chromed parts. Let the wax dry and wipe it off with a clean rag.

13. Use Bike Elixir or Simichrome to polish aluminum parts.

14. Reassemble the bike. If the chain was removed, lubricate it and wipe away the excess before reinstallation.

15. Use a spray lube such as Tri-Flow to lubricate the brake and derailleur pivots and all points where cables enter or exit housings and touch guides or stops. Also lubricate the chain if it remained on the bike during this cleaning.

Part Two

TIRES AND WHEELS

⬛6️⃣ CLINCHER TIRE REPAIR

A flat tire is one of those givens in life that occurs at the worst possible moment. To minimize its effect, learn to repair flats quickly. The procedure is easy to master.

Since patching tires with highway tar is virtually impossible, it's important to carry a repair kit. It should include:

- A spare tube (sized to your tire)
- Two or three tire levers
- A patch kit (for the inevitable second puncture)
- A frame-mounted pump, which should have either a Schrader valve (as found on auto tires) or a Presta valve (narrow, European) to match your tubes and spare

Removal and Inspection

Before beginning to repair a flat, find a safe place to work, away from traffic. Don't turn the bike upside down, because you might damage the brake cables or replace the wheel improperly. Rather, remove the wounded wheel, lay the bike on its left (nondrivetrain) side, and follow these steps.

1. Deflate the tube completely by depressing the spring-loaded center pin on a Schrader valve, or by unscrewing and depressing the pin on a Presta valve.

2. Insert the flat, spoonlike surface of one tire lever between the tire bead and the rim, about 2 inches from the valve. Pry off the bead by pulling the lever toward the hub and hooking it to a spoke. (See illustration 2-1.)

3. Insert a second lever under the same bead about 2 inches to the other side of the valve. Pull the lever down, prying off more of the bead. If the bead is still tight, hook this lever to a spoke and insert a third lever 2 inches farther along the rim. Then pry at 4-inch intervals until the entire bead is free. It's unnecessary to unseat the other bead from the rim to remove the tube.

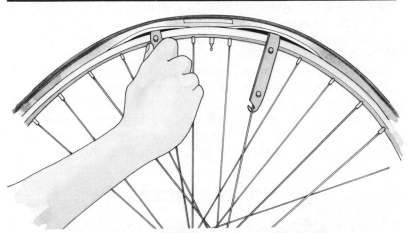

Illustration 2-1. Removing a tire with tire levers.

4. Starting opposite the valve, pull the inner tube from the tire. Then carefully remove the valve from the rim.

5. Locate the puncture by inflating the tube and listening for a hiss. Water or saliva rubbed on the leak will bubble.

6. Match the damaged part of the tube to the corresponding section of tire to find the cause of the puncture. Inspect the tire for holes, cut tread, or a detached bead. You might find a shard of glass or other sharp object lodged in the tread.

Remove all foreign matter and double-check by feeling under the tread. If the tire has a hole larger than ⅛ inch, you must repair it to contain the tube. A folded dollar bill works well in an emergency (it's linen, not paper). Just place it across the hole before installing the tube. Inflate only to 75 percent of recommended pressure.

Repairing the Tube

On the road, it's easier to install a spare, but if you have to repair the tube, follow these steps.

1. Choose the right patch. Small round ones work best on pinhole punctures, while long, oval patches fit the dual snake-bite holes made by a rim pinch. Blowouts of ½ inch or more are usually beyond repair.

2. Buff the area around the puncture with sandpaper. Make it slightly larger than the patch.

3. Apply a thin, even coat of glue to the buffed surface and allow it to dry (it will turn from shiny to dull).

4. Peel the backing from the patch and apply it carefully to the glued area, pressing it firmly in place (you only get one chance). Some patches have foil on one side and plastic on the other. The surface under the foil goes against the glue.

Reinstallation

1. Inflate the new or repaired tube until it just takes shape.

2. Insert the valve into the rim.

3. Carefully work the tube into the tire so there are no kinks or wrinkles.

4. Begin working the bead onto the rim, starting at the valve. Don't use tire levers for installation—you're likely to cause another puncture by pinching the tube.

5. As the bead becomes harder to push onto the rim, deflate the tube completely to provide maximum slack. Then, use the palms of your hands to push the bead into place.

6. Push the valve stem into the tire to ensure that the bead is seated, then pull out firmly.

7. Fully inflate the tire and spin the wheel in your hands as you watch the bead line on each side. It should appear just above the rim. If it bulges up or dips below, deflate the tube and use your hands to work the tire into place.

It's best to go through this procedure at least once at home so your roadside repairs will be quick and competent.

7 Pump Repair

Most cyclists learn pump maintenance the hard way. Just before an important ride, their floor pump won't put enough pressure in the tire or its head won't stay on the valve. Worse yet is a frame pump that malfunctions after a flat. But uncooperative pumps shouldn't be discarded. They can usually be repaired inexpensively, and if you know a few maintenance tricks you can prevent such problems from recurring.

There are many different types of pumps, including frame-fit, floor, and single and double chamber designs. They can be made of metal or plastic, but they all have similar mechanisms. Typically, the handle is connected to a plunger rod inside a cylinder. As the handle is pulled, the cylinder fills with air. When it's pushed, a leather or plastic cupped washer expands because of the air pressure being exerted upon it. This seals the washer against the inside of the cylinder and directs the air through the pump base, the hose (if any), the head, and into the inner tube.

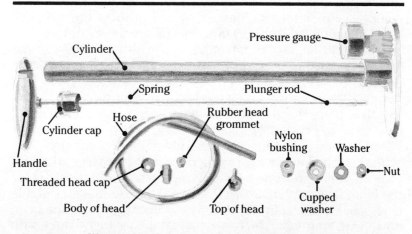

Illustration 2-2. Anatomy of a Silca pump.

Most air leaks occur because of a poor seal at the valve, a worn-out cupped washer, bad hose connections, loose pump components, or a bent or dented cylinder.

Only a few basic items are needed to repair a pump: pliers, flat-head screwdriver, a set of metric wrenches, and grease. You'll need a pair of diagonal cutters (or a sharp knife) and some small clamps to remedy hose problems. To find the trouble spot, listen closely while you work the pump. Or have a friend attempt to fill a tire while you search for the source of the escaping air.

Loose Valve Connection

For a pump to operate efficiently, its head must fit snugly over the inner tube valve. If it doesn't, the rubber grommet in the pump head is probably worn and/or dried out. Replacement grommets are available in bike shops.

1. Unscrew the cap on the pump head, pull out the old grommet, and drop in the new one. Other small parts may come out with the old grommet, so keep them in their original order.

2. Make sure the pump head hardware is not cracked or loose. Replace or tighten any problem pieces. Some pump heads will tightly fit the valve only when the grommet is compressed. Tightening the cap often improves the seal. Use thread-sealing (plumbing) tape to seal any leaky unions.

3. Occasionally a pump head will be difficult to press onto the valve. In this case, lubricate it with mild soap, talcum powder, or saliva. Don't use oil-based or silicone lubricants because the chemicals they contain can ruin rubber.

4. Replace the grommet once or twice a year, regardless of condition, to prevent problems.

V-section aero rims have created a unique leak problem. When matched with an aero rim, normal Presta valves may not protrude enough to be fully grasped by a pump head. Thus, the head leaks or blows off. Presta valve extenders, available in shops, are one solution. Another is to simply hold the head down with your foot. You can also tie the hose to the valve with a section of old inner tube. To do this, cut a slot in the middle of the tube section just large enough for the head to fit through.

Then place the head over the valve, wrap the ends of the tube over the tire, tie them in place, and pump.

Worn Hose

A floor pump hose will eventually wear out and fail. Usually the deterioration occurs where it connects with the pump base or head fitting. Although you can usually buy a replacement hose, you can save money by repairing the old one. (However, if there's a crack in the middle of the hose where it's been folded for storage, you'll have to replace it.)

1. Clip off the damaged section with diagonal cutters and reconnect the hose to the pump or pump head.

2. If the hose is held on with small, springlike wire clips, substitute little hose clamps. These last longer and make future repairs easier. They're available at hardware and auto parts stores.

Bad Washer

Washer failures are another cause of pump woes. When the cupped washer gets worn, it fails to catch the air and lets the plunger fall to the bottom of the pump without resistance. Sometimes the bolt that secures the washer to the plunger will loosen and permit it to fall off.

1. Unscrew the cap on the top of the cylinder. Wipe off the washer and work new grease into it. Don't use oil because it will get inside the inner tube and rot the rubber.

2. Flare the washer out so it barely fits back into the cylinder. If the washer won't hold its shape, replace it.

3. Make sure the washer retaining nut is snug before reassembly.

4. Check and lube the washer twice per season.

Dented Cylinder

Small dents or bends in the cylinder can also cause the cupped washer to leak. They can sometimes be pushed back out from the inside with a long screwdriver or a length of pipe. A crack or a severe dent or bend usually sends a pump to the bicycle accessory graveyard. Save the parts to repair your next pump, though.

Backfiring

One problem incorrectly attributed to pumps is "backfiring." This is when the pump handle jumps back suddenly, striking the user and/or breaking the pump. This is usually caused by an inner tube valve malfunction. It's most common with Presta valves. As the tire inflates, the valve gets stuck open, permitting the building pressure to shoot into the pump cylinder. You can prevent this by placing the pump head onto the valve just far enough to adequately grip it. Pushing it too far will depress the valve and cause backfire. Also, the valve should be kept clean and covered with a cap when not in use.

8 WHEEL TRUING

Truing bicycle wheels is not some arcane science reserved for experienced bike mechanics, aerospace engineers, or the most mechanically minded among us. It requires only a basic understanding of the process, and some practice. What's more, it's worth learning, because straight, evenly tensioned wheels are more reliable and allow a tighter brake adjustment.

Tools

The most important truing tool is a good wrench for turning the spoke nipples. There are different nipple sizes, but you needn't worry about this if you purchase an inexpensive multisize spoke wrench.

Truing is easiest in a wheel stand that lets you spin the wheel and inspect the rim for bends as it passes the adjustable reference arms (usually large bolts with easy-to-turn knobs). Truing stands are available from bike shops, beginning at about $40. In this discussion it's assumed that you are using such a stand. (Alternatively, you can hang or support your bike so the wheel being worked on is off the ground and turns freely. In this case, the brake pads are the reference points. If the wheel is so bent that it strikes the pads and cannot turn, open the brake quick-release to provide extra room.)

Since major wheel truing mistakes can be costly, you may want to practice on a used wheel. Ask at a shop for a cheap or free one. For this purpose, a wheel with significant wobbles is best because the bad spots are easily identified and improvements are more noticeable.

Inspection

Damaged wheel components make truing difficult. For instance, it's important that nipples turn freely. Sometimes the corners of the nipples, which are made of brass, have been rounded, which prevents gripping them with a spoke wrench. Damaged nipples should be replaced one at a time before you start truing. Corroded nipples may not turn. You can try applying penetrating oil, but usually the best solution is to have the wheel rebuilt with new spokes.

Certain types of rim damage can make wheel truing difficult or impossible. When the rim is bent from a severe impact or has numerous impact dents or bulges, spoke tension adjustments do little good.

Truing Procedure

Ideally, wheels should be true laterally (no wobbles) and vertically (no hops or flat spots). Lateral truing is easier and, in most cases, more important.

1. Spin the wheel slowly and watch for lateral movement relative to the reference points. Initially it's helpful to mark the wobbles by holding a felt-tip marker against one of the reference points.

2. Wiggle each spoke to find loose ones. Mark them or apply a piece of tape so they can be found later. It's likely that the loose spokes are near your rim marks.

3. Rotate the wheel so the loose spoke is at the truing stand's reference arms. Turn the nipple counterclockwise one-half turn at a time until it feels as tight as the other spokes when you wiggle it. (It's easy to get confused and turn the spoke nipple the wrong way. To prevent this, always bring nipples to the same position near the stand's arms at the bottom of the wheel before making adjustments. In this position, counterclockwise turns, as viewed from above, will tighten the spokes and clockwise turns will loosen them.) Repeat for the other loose spokes.

High-quality wheels are strong and durable because the spokes are evenly tensioned. While this is difficult to master quickly without a special, relatively expensive tool called a spoke tensiometer, adequate strength can be achieved by developing a feel for optimum tension and ensuring that there are no extremely loose spokes. If you spin the wheel now, you should notice that it's not quite as wobbly. Tightening the loose spokes made it straighter.

4. The next step is more truing to minimize lateral movement. This takes patience. Always adjust nipples a half turn at a time and spin the wheel to check progress. It may look like nothing happened, but if you keep working the wheel will improve.

On every wheel there are right- and left-side spokes. At the rim, the spokes are staggered to each side. The easiest way to tell which is a right or left spoke is to look at which hub flange it attaches to.

If you need to move a section of the rim to the left, you can tighten spokes leading from it to the left hub flange, loosen spokes leading to the right hub flange, or do a little of each. (See illustration 2-3.) Always feel for loose or tight spokes at the wobble, and take this into account when deciding what to do. Usually, tension differences correspond to the wobble in the rim, and correcting them should result in quick alignment. This may only require adjusting two to four nipples. Always strive for even tension.

Important: Keep in mind that the right spokes in a rear wheel are always tighter than those on the left due to rear wheel "dish." (Because of the space occupied by the freewheel, the rim must be closer to the right hub flange than the left in order to be centered in the frame.) Still, the spokes going to each flange should be equally tensioned among themselves.

True the largest wobble (the longest mark), then move to the next trouble spot. For instance, if the mark is on the right side of the rim, that part of the rim needs to move to the left. If the spokes feel evenly tensioned, loosen the right-side spokes in this area one-half turn and tighten the left-side spokes one-half turn. Check the result. Try to tighten or loosen several spokes at a time, and avoid using one spoke to pull the rim into true. Continue working until all wobbles are gone.

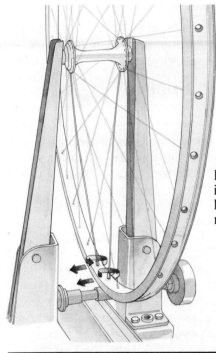

Illustration 2-3. Turn nipples as indicated to move rim to the left; turn in opposite direction to move to the right.

5. Eliminating vertical movement (putting a wheel into "round") may be more difficult. Spin the wheel and look for vertical movement relative to the reference arms. (The tire and tube must be removed.) Again, mark the problem spots. If the rim moves inward toward the hub (a "flat spot"), slightly loosen four consecutive spokes in that area. If the rim moves away from the hub ("hop"), tighten four spokes in that area. After each set of adjustments, check and correct for lateral movement. Keep in mind that it's normally not possible (or essential) to make a used wheel completely round.

Also, perfect vertical or lateral alignment will be impossible on your beat-up practice wheel. When it's as good as possible, you might want to loosen spokes at random and try truing it again. Then you'll feel confident enough to work on your own wheels.

■ 9 ■ SPOKE REPLACEMENT

Today's spokes are stronger than ever, but they still break. Here's how to remedy this occasional inconvenience.

Getting Home

For some unexplained reason, spokes seem to break when you're farthest from home. Telltale signs include a sudden loss of wheel trueness and/or the sound of a broken spoke striking fork blades or stays. If you don't have a spoke wrench in your tool kit, follow these steps.

1. Open the quick-release lever on the appropriate brake to allow for clearance of the wobbly rim.

2. Unscrew the threaded end of the broken spoke from the nipple, and slide the head from the hub. If the nipple won't yield or if the spoke head is trapped by the freewheel, bend the broken spoke around adjoining spokes to prevent it from snagging something and causing further damage.

3. Gingerly ride home. Excessive mileage or impact on a wheel with a broken spoke can permanently damage your rim.

If you're carrying a spoke wrench, loosen the two spokes on either side of the broken one so the rim becomes straight enough to clear the brake pads. Don't overdo it, though. Self-reliant cyclists with spare spokes and proper tools can follow the rest of the instructions for a complete roadside repair.

Getting Ready

Most bike shops stock spokes in lengths ranging from 280 to 308 mm. They come in 1 or 2mm increments and several different gauges. It's best to have your ailing wheel with you when spoke shopping. Next best is the broken spoke itself, and detailed information about lacing pattern, hub and rim brand or model, and the number of spokes the wheel *should* have. "It's for a blue 10-speed," isn't enough information for a mechanic to precisely match spokes.

Once you find the correct replacement spoke, buy several so you're ready for the next twang. Also, buy a quality spoke wrench that fits the nipples on your bike. A carefully wielded 6-inch adjustable wrench will work in a pinch.

If a spoke breaks on the freewheel side of the rear wheel (the most common location) you'll also need a freewheel removal tool or a pair of chainwhips (for cassette hubs) to access the hub flange. It's also easier to replace broken spokes on the left side of the rear wheel if the freewheel is removed. Here's how it's done.

1. Remove the rear wheel from the bike.

2. Remove the freewheel-side axle nut or quick-release skewer nut.

3. Slip the freewheel removal tool over the axle and into the freewheel body. (Illustration 2-4 shows common tools.)

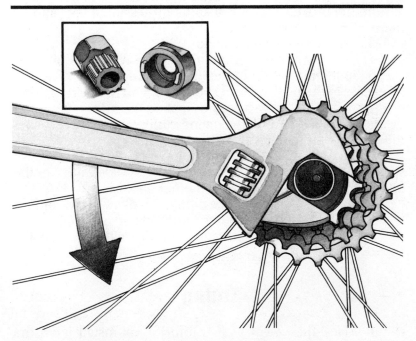

Illustration 2-4. Freewheel removal tools.

4. Thread on the axle or skewer nut snugly to hold the tool in place.

5. Fit a large adjustable wrench to the removal tool or, better yet, clamp it in a bench vise.

6. Turn the wrench or wheel counterclockwise until the freewheel just breaks loose from the hub threads.

7. Remove the axle nut or quick-release skewer nut holding the removal tool in place.

8. Continue carefully unscrewing the freewheel until it's completely off the hub.

(For instructions on removing cassette hub cogs, see chapter 18.)

Replacement

1. Remove the tire, tube, and rim strip (or tubular tire) from the wheel.

2. Inspect the rim for dents, cracks, or other damage around the broken spoke. Consult a professional bike shop if there's anything suspicious.

3. Remove the broken spoke.

4. Lube the threads of the new spoke with light oil.

5. Slide the spoke into the hub from the proper direction (opposite to the two adjacent spokes). If you're inserting from outside to inside, gently curve the spoke's threaded end toward the rim in order to keep it from being obstructed as it approaches the spokes on the opposite side.

6. Lace the spoke to the rim. Usually, it goes under two spokes and over the third, or under three spokes and over the fourth. Imitate the pattern of the other spokes.

7. Screw on the new spoke nipple. It's okay if three or four spoke threads are exposed on the hub side of the nipple when it's finger-tight, but if any threads protrude on the tire side, the spoke is too long.

Truing

1. Place the wheel in a truing jig, or install it on the bike for truing. In either case, your goal is to have the wheel spin freely.

2. When truing on the bike, cock the brake caliper to one side so the part of the rim that's straight skims the surface of the brake pad, while the lumpy section swings away.

3. The object of truing is to make the rim run straight (no hops or wobbles) due to equal tension in each spoke connected to the same hub flange. (Freewheel-side spokes are tighter than those on the opposite side.)

4. If you didn't loosen the two spokes adjoining the broken one, you can usually true the wheel by simply turning the new spoke nipple counterclockwise until that portion of the rim runs smoothly past the brake pad.

5. If you did loosen the two adjoining spokes, you'll have to tighten them (and the new spoke) to make the wheel round and smooth running. Start by tightening the new spoke nipple until the rim runs smoothly past the brake pad. Then pluck all three spokes and compare their tone to others on the wheel. (Remember, spokes on the freewheel side have a higher tone than their counterparts.) Tighten the two loose spokes and the new spoke one-quarter turn each while comparing tones. Don't worry about achieving concert quality—just make them sound similar.

6. Spin the wheel again to check your work. Does the rim run consistently past the brake pad? Hold a ruler against the seatstays or fork blades about ⅛ inch above the rim. If the rim hops up or down more than ⅛ inch, you have an involved truing job.

7. Lightly grease the freewheel's threads and carefully install it on the hub. Begin in a counterclockwise direction to align the threads, then reverse direction. After you snug it by hand, riding the bike will take care of final tightening.

8. Reinstall the rim strip, tire, and tube (or tubular tire).

Sometimes a broken spoke is a sign of wheel fatigue. If broken spokes become a recurring problem, your wheel should be rebuilt with new spokes.

■10■ EASY RIM REPLACEMENT

Many cyclists consider wheelbuilding an art that's best left to the pros. One reason for this is the difficulty of lacing spokes. Fortunately, there is a way to skip this step entirely. If your spokes are sound and an identical replacement rim is available (same size and brand), you can rebuild your wheel without entirely removing the spokes. Thus, you needn't know a thing about lacing.

Tools

To replace a rim, you'll need the proper size spoke wrench, electrical tape, a flat-head screwdriver, tire levers, oil (linseed, Wheelsmith Spoke Prep, Tri-Flow, or the like), a new rim, and a few new spokes if some are damaged. If rear spokes require replacing, you'll also need a freewheel remover. A truing stand and dishing gauge are helpful, but you can improvise by using your brake pads and frame as reference points. A tensiometer (gauge for checking spoke tension) is also useful but not necessary.

Inspection

Spokes become prone to breakage with age, so you should inspect them carefully. Squeeze a pair of crossed spokes so they separate, and view the junction where they've been rubbing. If there is a deep groove, the spokes need replacing. Also, rusty spokes may break and should be discarded. Nipples should turn freely and show no signs of corrosion.

Spoke lengths vary in 1mm increments, and the proper size depends on several factors, including rim shape. Thus, when purchasing a rim you should take your wheel to the shop in order to get the same brand, model, size, and number of spoke holes. If you can't locate an identical replacement, ask a shop mechanic to find one with the same dimensions using a spoke chart.

If a different brand is to be used, check its spoke-hole orientation. Most rims have offset holes, meaning that every other hole is closer to one side of the rim. To check this, rest the new rim atop the old wheel with the valve holes aligned. Inspect the spoke hole to the right of the valve on each rim. The offset should be to the same side.

Correction

If a wheel is warped or "pretzeled," it can be difficult to transfer the spokes. Hence, you must straighten the rim as much as possible beforehand.

Start by loosening all the spokes. Spin the wheel and note where the rim is badly warped and in which direction it needs to be bent. Place the bad spot over your knee and pull it into shape (as if you were breaking kindling for a fire).

An alternative is the slam method. Do this with the tire and tube in place. Locate the bad spot. Holding the wheel with both hands, strike it against the floor. Start gently and increase the strength of the blow until the rim is fairly straight.

Replacement

1. Remove the tire, tube, and rim strip.

2. If spokes are to be replaced in the rear wheel, remove the freewheel.

Illustration 2-5. Taping the new rim to the old one allows foolproof spoke transfer.

3. Loosen all the nipples, but don't remove them.

4. Replace damaged spokes as necessary, being careful to duplicate their orientation in the hub (head in or head out) and the way they cross other spokes.

5. Tape the new rim to the old in six to eight places, with the valve holes aligned.

6. Starting next to the valve hole, transfer each spoke to the new rim. Use a screwdriver on the head of the nipple (inside the rim) to speed the process. Engage the nipples two turns.

7. Put a drop of oil on the spoke threads and in each nipple pocket of the new rim.

Truing

This is the important part, so take your time. Don't add too much tension until the new rim is round and true. It's easy to be overzealous. However, rotating a nipple one turn can have a major effect on the shape of your wheel. Always use a half turn or less and check its effect.

1. Put the wheel in your truing stand or frame. (With the latter, prop the bike so you can spin the wheel.)

2. Tighten each spoke equally with a screwdriver using the number of exposed threads as a gauge. To properly dish a rear wheel that uses the same spoke length throughout, leave several threads exposed on spokes leading to the left side of the hub, and none on spokes leading to the freewheel side. A wheel using slightly shorter spokes on the freewheel side should be tightened to expose the same number of threads throughout.

3. Check trueness by spinning the wheel and viewing the rim's position relative to the brake pads or the arms of a truing stand. You may find it helpful to hold a felt-tip marker next to the rim and mark out-of-true spots as they pass.

In those places where the rim needs to move right, tighten one or two spokes leading to the right side of the hub, and loosen one or two spokes leading to the left side of the hub. (Make these adjustments in quarter turns, then spin the wheel and repeat if necessary.) To move the rim to the left, do the opposite. Tightening and loosening equal numbers of spokes will ensure that the wheel remains round. True the wheel with very little spoke tension before moving to the next step.

4. Spin the wheel to check for vertical movement (roundness). Place a pencil across the brake pads and view the rim as it passes underneath, or use the arms of the truing stand as reference points. If a section of the rim is high, tighten four spokes in that area (two from each side). If the rim is low (a flat spot), loosen. Emphasize loosening rather than tightening, and work in pairs.

5. Repeat steps 3 and 4 until the rim is true and round.

6. Using both hands (one on each side of the wheel), squeeze pairs of spokes gently to seat the nipples.

7. Add tension. For a front wheel, tighten every spoke a half turn. For a rear wheel, tighten the freewheel-side spokes a half turn and the left-hand spokes a quarter turn.

8. Check wheel dish. This is correct when the rim is centered between the axle locknuts. It ensures that the wheel will be aligned within the frame.

Follow the manufacturer's instructions when using a dishing gauge. Otherwise, flip the wheel over in the frame periodically and check the rim's position relative to the brake pads. It should be the same distance from them regardless of wheel orientation. To alter dish, tighten all spokes on one side of the wheel a quarter turn to pull the rim to that side. Check and repeat if necessary.

9. Continue adding tension, squeezing spokes and adjusting for trueness and roundness until the proper tension is achieved. A tensiometer is the most accurate way to check for this. Alternatively, squeeze spokes and compare their tension to that of another wheel, or pluck the spokes and compare their tone. In general, it's better to err on the side of looseness. A shop mechanic can also check the tension. Remember that left-hand spokes on rear wheels are looser than those on the freewheel side.

Part Three
BRAKES

![11] SERVICING CALIPER BRAKES

Riders who've had the misfortune of snapping a brake cable know it usually happens when you need the brakes the most—during a panic stop. You can avoid the consequences with frequent inspection and periodic replacement of cables and housings. Here's how to do it for the sidepull caliper brakes found on most road bikes.

Inspection

Cables invariably break at the end button, the metal bulb that holds the cable in the brake lever. On all standard levers and most aero levers (concealed cables) you can see the end button when you squeeze the lever and look into the opening.

Loose wire strands at the end button mean the cable is breaking. Also, if the cable just above the button looks brighter than the rest, the button may be slipping off. In either case, replace the cable.

If the cable housing has kinks or crimps, it should be replaced as well. Besides wearing the cable, this reduces braking sensitivity because of increased friction. On standard brakesets, examine the housing where it enters the top of the lever. This portion can be easily kinked if the bike is carried in a car or if you turn the bike upside down for repair work (a good reason never to do this).

Several brake manufacturers recommend annual cable and housing replacement as a precaution. This is one instance where if it ain't broke, fix it anyway.

To avoid duplicating work, replace worn brake pads and handlebar tape, and true your wheels at the time you replace and adjust your brake cables.

Removal

1. With aero levers, unwrap the handlebar tape and any adhesive tape holding the cable housing to the handlebar.

2. Remove the top tube brake cable clips if your bike has these rather than brazed-on tunnels.

3. Loosen each brake's cable anchor bolt and pull out the cable. This usually requires an 8mm wrench or 4mm Allen key.

4. Remove each cable from the bike, pulling it through or unhooking it from the lever, as necessary. If the cable end button is stuck, reach into the lever with needle-nose pliers, grip the cable slightly above the button, and push it down.

5. Remove both cable housings. Don't lose the small metal caps that may be at each end.

Installation

Replace worn cables and housing with the identical brand. Or, if you have inexpensive brakes, you can improve their performance by installing thicker cables and housing with a low-friction liner. Consult your dealer.

1. Use diagonal cutters to size the new housing to the old. Finish the ends with a fine file. This eliminates excess friction and wear at these points and provides a stable base against which the housing can compress.

2. Lubricate the entire cable (especially the end button) with quality waterproof bike grease or a viscous oil. This reduces friction and prevents rust.

3. Hook each cable end button into its lever and slide on the housing. Make sure the housing and buttons are fully seated and remain so during adjustment. Remember, it is standard for the left lever to operate the front brake.

4. Thread the rear housing through the top tube tunnels or install the cable clips—not so tight they flatten the housing.

5. Insert each cable into its brake anchor bolt. Do not tighten.

6. If you have aero levers, tape the housing to the handlebar in three places with nylon-reinforced tape. This holds it in place and reduces strain on the handlebar tape. Shimano offers a plastic "caterpillar," which covers the housing and eliminates pressure by the tape.

Adjustment

1. On each brake, screw in the barrel adjuster all the way, then unscrew it one turn. Do the same on each lever if they have adjusters.

2. Hold the brake pads against the rim with a third-hand tool or a toe strap. (See illustration 3-1.)

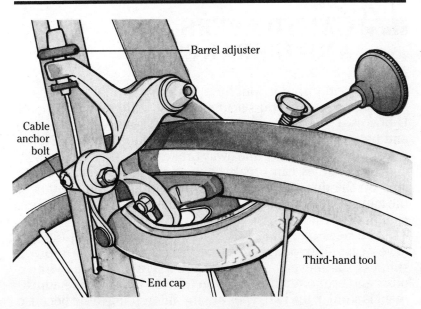

Illustration 3-1. Using a third-hand tool.

3. Pull the cable taught with a pair of pliers and tighten the cable anchor bolt.

4. Firmly squeeze the brake lever ten times to compress and seat the cable housing and make sure the cable doesn't slip through the anchor bolt.

5. Remove cable slack by duplicating step 3, then repeat step 4.

6. Remove the third-hand tool or strap, snap the brake lever a couple of times, then check the distance between the brake pads and the rim. Turn the barrel adjuster to make the gap about 2 mm.

7. Finish by soldering the cable end to prevent it from fraying, or use a crimp-on or slide-on cap.

This maintenance procedure should keep your brake cable/housing system in top shape for at least a year. But don't take your safety for granted. Get in the habit of inspecting the cable ends and squeezing the brake levers hard before every ride.

12 CANTILEVERS AND U-BRAKES

Off-road riding is tough on brakes, and that's why most mountain bikes use powerful stoppers—either cantilevers or U-brakes. These offer more clearance (for wide, muddy tires) and better performance and durability than sidepulls. None-theless, it's possible to grind away brake pads on a long descent, and main cables can break, causing the transverse cable to land on the tire, stopping the wheel and launching you over the handlebar. Ouch. Regular maintenance, as described here, can prevent such mishaps.

U-brakes (see illustration 3-2) resemble centerpulls but have heavy-duty parts and mount to frame posts to improve stiffness. Cantilevers (see illustration 3-3) also mount to frame posts and are sometimes used on touring bikes. While adjust-ment is similar, the two types are not interchangeable because the frame posts are in different positions.

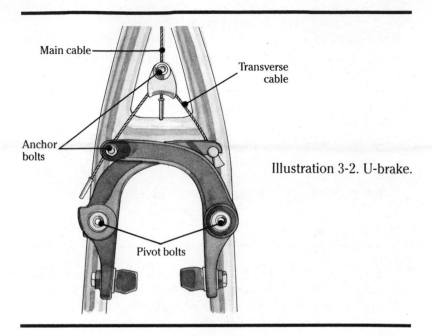

Main cable

Transverse
cable

Anchor
bolts

Pivot bolts

Illustration 3-2. U-brake.

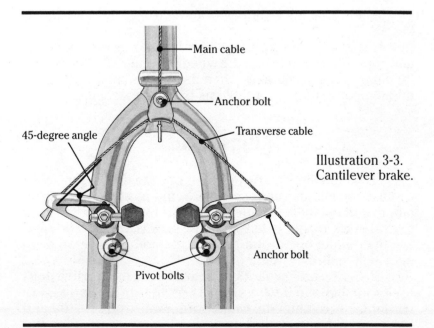

Main cable

Anchor bolt

45-degree angle

Transverse cable

Illustration 3-3.
Cantilever brake.

Anchor bolt

Pivot bolts

Tools and Materials

You'll need 8, 9, 10, and 17mm open-end wrenches; 2, 4, 5, and 6mm Allen wrenches; a third-hand tool (or toe strap); diagonal cutter; cable cutter; pliers; WD-40; thread adhesive; cable end caps; medium emery cloth; and grease.

Preparation

1. Clean the brakes with a rag and solvent. Check for worn pads. The grooves should be visible and the holders should not be in danger of contacting the rim. Check the cables for rust and fraying and the housing for cracks. Replace any worn parts.

2. Unscrew the pivot bolts and remove the calipers from the frame. If one arm is stuck, apply WD-40 and twist as you pull. Lightly sand the posts with emery cloth and apply a small amount of grease to their outer surface and the internal brake parts.

3. Lubricate the lever pivots and screw in the adjustment barrels.

4. Spin the wheels and look for lateral movement, dents, and hops. Check to see that the wheel is centered in the frame. It's difficult to adjust brakes when the wheels are out of true or misaligned, so fix these problems before proceeding.

Adjustment

1. Mount the arms on the posts one at a time so you won't confuse the left and right springs. Some models have spring tabs that fit into holes on the braze-on. Occasionally there are several holes for spring tension adjustments. If this is the case, use the middle one. Put a drop of thread adhesive on each pivot bolt and screw them in.

2. Set the preliminary spring tension on models that don't use spring holes in the frame posts. Most U-brake springs are tensioned by rotating the caliper arm away from the rim and tightening the pivot bolt. The farther the arm is from the rim when tightened, the greater the spring tension.

New cantilever models and Dia-Compe U-brakes employ a 17mm tensioning nut that is locked in place with the pivot bolt. To add tension to U-brakes, the right tensioning nut is turned counterclockwise and the left, clockwise. Cantilever models are the opposite. Tension the brake arms evenly by rotating the nut one-eighth turn at a time, tightening the pivot bolt, and moving the arm by hand to check the adjustment. You shouldn't have to use more than one-half turn total.

Some older Dia-Compe cantilevers use exposed springs that wrap around the brake pad hardware. Temporarily unhook the spring by hand to make cable adjustment easier.

3. Grease the cable and its soldered-on head. If your bike has a bottom bracket cable guide for a chainstay-mounted U-brake, grease it. Trim the housing so it's long enough to allow full handlebar movement but not so long that the brakes feel spongy. If the housing fits loosely in the frame stops or brake hangers, install metal end caps called ferrules (available from bike shops).

4. Connect the transverse cable clamp to the cable 2 inches above the tire and tighten it so it can be moved by hand but won't slide on its own.

On Shimano Deore XT cantilevers, the brake cable passes through a round transverse cable clamp on its way to an anchor bolt on one brake arm. The transverse cable has three soldered-on fittings. Attach one end to the brake arm and the middle fitting to the transverse cable clamp. This leaves one fitting and a short piece of exposed cable that can be gripped and pulled for use as a quick-release. Snug the anchor bolts on the transverse cable clamp and brake arm.

On chainstay-mounted U-brakes, pull the end of the brake cable and slide the transverse cable clamp against the bottom bracket guide. Pull the lever to the handlebar. This will cause the clamp to slide to the correct position on the cable. Tighten it there.

5. Thread the transverse cable through the transverse cable clamp and place its ends in the brake arm slots. If there is an anchor bolt on one side, loosen it and insert the transverse cable.

Cantilever transverse cables should form a 45-degree angle with the brake arms. Hold the brake pads against the rim with a third-hand tool or toe strap. Slide the transverse cable clamp on the brake cable, and the transverse cable through the anchor bolts (if applicable) until the angle is correct. Tighten the anchor bolts.

On Shimano Deore XT cantilevers, the distance from the transverse cable clamp to each brake arm should be identical. Slide the clamp on the brake cable as needed, and tighten the anchor bolts.

On U-brakes, the transverse cable clamp should already be tight on the brake cable. Use a third-hand tool or toe strap to hold the pads against the rim. Pull up the transverse cable and place it in the transverse cable clamp. Tighten the anchor bolt.

6. Cantilever and U-brakes move the pads toward the rim in an arc. If the pads aren't carefully positioned, they can strike the tire or pass under the rim and go into the spokes. (The latter can also be caused by excessive pad wear.) Operate the brakes to ensure that the full surface of the pads strikes the rim and they're slightly toed-in. (The front of the pad should touch the rim first to prevent squealing.) Left and right brake pad position should be identical.

Two types of pads are used on cantilevers and U-brakes: bolt-on and post-mounted. Both have special washers that are rotated to toe-in the pads. Once positioned, secure the pad by securing its holder with an Allen wrench while tightening the mounting nut. If the pad is a bolt-on type, grasp the pad with pliers while tightening the nut.

Reattach Dia-Compe brake springs.

7. Pull the levers hard to stretch the cables and test brake pad tightness. Readjust and tighten if necessary.

8. Adjust the cables so there is ⅛ inch of clearance between the rim and pads, and tighten the anchor bolts. Cut the cables one inch past the anchors and install end caps to prevent fraying.

9. Center the brakes by adjusting spring tension. First, operate each brake and note if one side is dragging on the rim once the lever is released. If so, spring tension must be increased on this side.

Spring tension on cantilevers can be increased by disconnecting the transverse cable and rotating the arm away from the rim. This unwinds the spring and effectively increases tension. It's usually necessary to do this several times.

Tension adjustments on cantilevers with multiple spring holes are made by moving the spring to another hole.

U-brake (and some new cantilever) tension adjustments are made by loosening the pivot bolt, turning the spring adjuster or brake arm, and locking it in place with the pivot bolt. Some brakes have 2mm Allen bolts on one side that make minor tension adjustments simple. Turning the bolt counterclockwise reduces spring tension and allows the other arm to move away from the rim. Turning it clockwise has the opposite effect.

10. Test the brakes for squealing and increase toe-in if necessary. If the noise persists, sand the rims lightly with emery cloth.

Part Four

GEAR SYSTEM

■ 13 INSTALLING AND ADJUSTING AN INDEX SHIFTING SYSTEM

Index rear derailleurs have made shifting easier, faster, and more accurate. However, the convenience of these "click" systems comes with a small cost. It's more important to install parts carefully and make occasional cable adjustments than it was with old-style "friction" systems.

Here are guidelines for installing and adjusting index rear derailleur systems. If your bike already has indexing and you simply need to adjust it, skip the section entitled, "Installation of Components."

Frame Alignment

A correctly aligned frame is essential for indexing. The dropouts must be aligned and the derailleur hanger must be parallel to the bike's centerline. The distance between the inside surfaces of the rear dropouts should be at least 126 mm. If you doubt your frame is correct, have a bike shop do the checks because special tools are required.

Some derailleur hangers cause index systems to work poorly. For best shifting, the derailleur's upper pulley should stay close to the freewheel cogs. If the distance between the center of the rear axle and the center of the derailleur mounting bolt is more than 1¼ inches you may get poor indexing, particularly when shifting among the small cogs.

Installation of Components

Index components work best as "systems." If possible, use the same brand and model of shift lever, freewheel, and rear derailleur. Most index "kits" also come with a chain, cables, and housing.

For installation you'll need cable cutters, a chain rivet tool, a freewheel remover for your particular freewheel, 4, 5, and 6mm Allen keys, screwdrivers, 8 and 9mm wrenches, hub cone wrenches, and a large adjustable wrench.

1. Remove the old shift lever, rear derailleur, chain, freewheel, cable, and housing. You may have to cut stubborn grips from mountain bike handlebars to remove the shifter.

2. Install the new lever. On a mountain bike, simply slide the new shifter on and tighten the mounting bolts. Install the brake lever and grip.

Mounting a down tube shifter requires more care. Usually the lever is mounted on a brazed-on frame fitting. Apply a little grease to the mounting bolt and internal lever parts, then screw the new lever to the braze-on. Note that Shimano Index System (SIS) right levers are not attached with the external D-ring but with a screw that sits inside the ring. (The D-ring switches the system from index to friction mode.) If the mounting bolt won't screw in smoothly or won't tighten enough to hold the lever, you may need to have a qualified mechanic tap out the braze-on threads.

3. Grease the derailleur mounting bolt and carefully screw the derailleur to the hanger using an Allen key. You may have to pull the derailleur back (toward the rear of the bike) to get it to screw in against the hanger.

4. Before installing the freewheel, check to see that the hub bearings are adjusted properly. (The axle should turn freely but have no up-and-down play.) The axle locknuts should be tight. Loose axle parts can change the spacing of the rear hub and affect indexing.

5. Lightly grease the freewheel's threads and carefully screw it onto the hub by hand. It should go on easily. If it doesn't, you may have cross-threaded it. Remove it and try again. (You may need a freewheel tool and adjustable wrench to get it off.) Once you have the freewheel threaded correctly, tighten it.

If you have a cassette freehub or integral hub and freewheel assembly, simply slide the cassette over the splined portion of the hub. The cassette is held in place by one or two threaded cogs (the smallest ones). Screw them on tightly. Be sure the orientation of the threaded cogs is correct—the amount of space between all adjacent cogs should be the same.

6. Install the wheel. Be sure the rim is centered between the chainstays and that the axle is mounted as far forward as possible in the dropouts. This helps position the freewheel close to the upper derailleur pulley.

7. Install the new chain. Often, a stiff link occurs where the chain is joined. Work the kink out by bending the chain back and forth with your hands.

To check for correct chain length, put it on the large chainring and the smallest cog. Looking from the right side, an

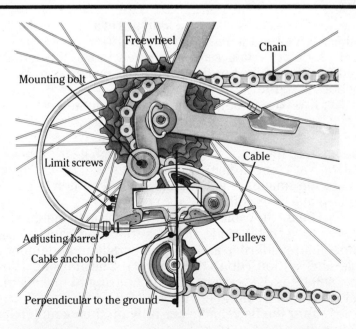

Illustration 4-1. Determining proper chain length.

imaginary line through the center of the derailleur pulleys should be perpendicular to the ground. If it isn't, add or remove a link as necessary.

Adjustment

1. Put the bike in a repair stand or suspend it so the crank can be turned.

2. Set the two derailleur limit screws before installing the cable. These govern how far the derailleur travels laterally and keep the chain from overshifting into the spokes or falling between the smallest cog and the right dropout.

Facing the right side of the bike, rotate the crank with your right hand. At the same time, push the body of the derailleur away from you with your left thumb, causing the chain to shift to the largest cog. If the chain goes over the freewheel into the spokes, turn the screw marked L (for "low gear") clockwise a half turn at a time until the problem is corrected. If the chain won't go onto the largest cog, turn the same screw counterclockwise a half turn at a time until it does. (If the screws are not marked, the lower or rearmost screw is usually L. To be certain, see which screw moves the derailleur when it's in its resting position under the smallest cog. The one that does is H; the opposite is L.)

Next, as you turn the crank, allow the derailleur to spring back to its resting position. The chain should go smoothly onto the smallest cog. If the chain goes past the cog and into the dropout, turn the screw marked H (for "high gear") clockwise a half turn at a time until it no longer does so. If the chain won't go onto the smallest cog, turn the screw counterclockwise a half turn at a time until it does.

3. Grease the cable lightly. Route it through the shift lever, bottom bracket cable guide, chainstay braze-on, cable housing, knurled barrel adjuster, and into the derailleur and under the cable anchor bolt (don't tighten yet). The housing should curve smoothly. If you must cut the housing to make a more gradual bend, be sure to file the end flat.

4. Turn the barrel adjuster fully in, then counterclockwise two turns. This provides some leeway for cable tension adjustments.

5. With the chain on the smallest cog and the shift lever fully forward, pull the cable taut with your hand as you tighten the anchor bolt, being careful not to move the derailleur from its resting position. The anchor bolt usually has a groove for the cable. Be sure the cable remains seated in this groove.

6. Check your limit screw adjustments by shifting the derailleur with the lever set in friction mode. (Read your instructions to determine how to make the mode change.)

7. Listen to the drivetrain as you turn the crank while in the largest and smallest cogs. There should be no rattling in-between-gears noises. Next, view the derailleur and pulleys from behind while in each of these two gears. The pulleys should be directly under the largest and smallest cogs.

8. Shift hard to the largest cog several times to stretch the new cable, then shift back to the small cog. Check the cable in the middle of the down tube to see that it's taut. If not, repeat the cable tightening procedure (step 5) and recheck the limit screw adjustments.

9. Check the indexing. Switch the lever to index mode and use your right hand to shift to the smallest cog while turning the crank with your left. Shift one click to the second smallest cog. The chain should instantly move to it and stay there. If it does not advance, turn the barrel adjuster counterclockwise a half turn and try the shift again. Continue making the adjustment a half turn at a time until the system shifts quickly and precisely.

10. Try the other cogs. Can you shift cleanly through the gears? Is the system free of rattling noises? If the answer to either question is no, try this technique: Shift to the second smallest cog. Continue to spin the crank and turn the barrel counterclockwise until you hear a rattling noise indicating the system is about to shift to the next larger cog. At this point, turn the barrel clockwise a small amount at a time until the noise disappears. This should tension the cable properly and produce good shifting over all the cogs.

If gear changes become less precise as the miles go by, the remedy is usually as simple as a half turn (counterclockwise) of the barrel adjuster to increase cable tension.

■14■ GEAR SYSTEM TUNE-UP

Got those noisy gear changer blues? Even the best systems require occasional cleaning and adjustment to continue operating smoothly and quietly. It's the condition and quality of cables, housing, chain, freewheel, and chainrings that determine shifting performance. Here's how to restore your system to like-new performance.

Cleaning

Excessive crud on the chain, derailleurs, and between freewheel cogs hinders shifting. Here's a quick way to floss and lube these components.

1. Lean the right side of the bike against a wall or fencepost, and position a wide, shallow pan beneath the drivetrain. (Keep the bike leaning on its right side to prevent degreaser from seeping into the bottom bracket or rear hub.)

2. Apply an automotive degreaser such as Gumout Engine Brite to the derailleurs, chain, and freewheel with a soft bottle brush. Work the degreaser between the freewheel cogs and all other nooks and crannies. Let it set for 5 to 10 minutes.

3. Rinse away the degreaser with a gentle stream of water from a bucket or garden hose. Repeat degreasing, if necessary.

4. When all the components are dry, apply a drop or spritz of your favorite lubricant to each chain link, derailleur pivot point, and the rear derailleur pulleys. Wipe away the excess with a clean rag.

Cables and Housing

Two great spinoff innovations of index shifting are stretch-resistant cables and compression-resistant housing. These items will enliven any sluggish shifter, and annual replacement ensures optimum performance from the systems for which they were designed.

1. Loosen the cable anchor bolt on each derailleur with

the appropriate tool (usually a 4, 5, or 6mm Allen key, or 8mm socket).

2. Pull the cables from the derailleurs, housing, and shift levers. You may need a pair of pliers to push the cable end buttons out of the levers. A drop of penetrating oil on a stuck button will help free it. If you intend to reuse the cables, trim any frayed ends with a cable cutter. This will ease reinsertion after cleaning.

3. Lube the end buttons of the new cables with a light film of bike grease. Lube the rest of the cable by running it through a cake of paraffin, or spray it with pure silicone. Both methods discourage dirt buildup.

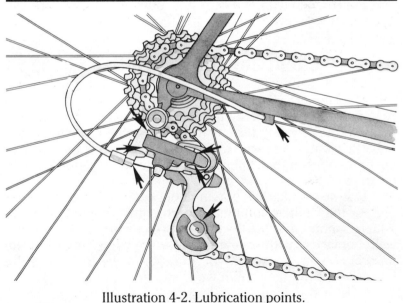

Illustration 4-2. Lubrication points.

4. If you're using compression-resistant housing, buy it in the length(s) needed. Otherwise, trim the housing to length with cable or diagonal cutters. Then snip the plastic covering 1 mm from the end of the metal inner casing, and file the metal flat. Cover the housing ends with ferrules where they meet the shift levers (on mountain bikes), frame-mounted stops, and derailleur(s).

5. Insert the cables into the shift levers, through the housing, guides, and stops, and into the derailleur. Move both levers all the way forward (road bike) or backward (mountain bike), pull the cables taut, and secure them with the derailleur cable anchor bolts.

6. Without pedaling, pull or push on each lever to seat and compress the housing and prestretch the cable. Then return the levers to their original resting position.

7. Loosen the derailleur cable anchor bolts, pull out the cable slack, and retighten. Prestretch the cables again as in step 6 to make sure they're secure.

8. Trim the cable ends to roughly 1 inch with cable cutters. Finish them with end caps or a touch of solder to prevent fraying.

Chain and Rear Derailleur

Chain length affects shifting performance in two ways: (1) An excessively worn chain has too much space between links to mesh properly with the cog teeth; (2) a chain with too many or too few links can result in delayed or missed shifts because the derailleur's upper pulley won't be properly oriented with the cogs.

1. A new chain has one inch between links (every other pin). Count 12 links and measure from the first pin to the last. If there's more than 12⅛ inches, your chain is too worn to shift well. Replace it with a new chain of the same model. If the freewheel teeth are worn, you may also have to replace the freewheel so the new chain won't slip under load.

2. Rear derailleurs are designed to work in a particular orientation to the freewheel cogs. Chain length partially determines this orientation. Generally, better shifting results when the upper derailleur pulley is closer to the freewheel cogs. Here's how to achieve this with some specific brands.

Campagnolo. Campy rear derailleurs usually work best with a maximum-length chain. With the chain on the smallest ring and cog, there should be minimum tension on the lower derailleur pulley. In other words, the chain should almost sag.

Shimano. For the best derailleur performance, put the

chain on the largest ring and smallest cog. In this position, size the chain so a line through the derailleur pulleys is perpendicular to the ground.

SunTour. New SunTour rear derailleurs have a notch on the body that aligns with an arrow on the pulley cage when a properly sized chain is on the largest ring and smallest cog. With older models, use the Shimano sizing method.

Freewheel

Worn freewheel cogs result in slower, less-accurate shifting. Inspect each cog for cracks and chipped teeth. Replace any that skip after a new chain is installed. (See chapter 16.) Use only equipment that's compatible with your system.

Some hubs position certain freewheels outside the range of some rear derailleurs. It's risky mixing hub, freewheel, and derailleur brands. Minor adjustments can be made by moving hub axle spacers and redishing the wheel, or by using shims behind the freewheel. If you can't get your derailleur to reach the inner or outermost cog, consult a pro mechanic.

Front Derailleur

To adjust cage proximity and alignment with the chainrings, front derailleurs can be pivoted and slid vertically on the seat tube. Proper orientation with the chainrings is essential for good shifting.

1. Loosen the cable anchor bolt and free the cable.

2. Loosen the front derailleur mounting bracket with the appropriate tool (usually a 4, 5, or 6mm Allen key, or 8mm socket).

3. Adjust the derailleur's position until the outside cage plate is parallel to the big chainring and clears it vertically by about 1 mm. For variations in cage alignment, refer to manufacturer's instructions. Shimano offers a gauge for aligning its indexed front derailleurs.

4. Tighten the mounting bracket bolt and recheck cage alignment. Make any necessary adjustments.

5. Reconnect the front derailleur cable (steps 5, 6, and 7 under "Cables and Housing") and make sure the outer cage plate clears the outer chainring when shifting. Readjust if necessary.

6. To check performance, make numerous shifts between the small and large chainrings. Try this with the chain on various freewheel cogs. Shifts should be clean with no hesitation or tendency to overshift.

7. If the chain goes over the large ring and around the crankarm, or if the crankarm touches the derailleur cage on each revolution, tighten the front derailleur's high-gear adjustment screw. This may be marked *H*; if not, it is usually the outer of the two screws. Tighten a half turn at a time until the problem is corrected and the chain still passes cleanly through the cage when coming from the smallest cog.

8. If the chain won't climb smartly onto the large ring, back off the high-gear adjustment screw until it will.

9. If the chain falls off the inside of the small chainring when you shift to it from the large one, tighten the other (low-gear) adjustment screw until the problem stops. Make sure the chain still passes cleanly through the cage when the chain is on the largest freewheel cog and the front derailleur shift lever is fully forward (road bike) or back (mountain bike).

10. If the chain won't drop quickly onto the small ring, back off the low-gear screw to move the derailleur cage inward. If it doesn't move when you do this and the shift lever is in its resting position, the cable is too tight. Open the fixing bolt to relieve tension, then retighten.

Alignment

A misaligned frame and especially a bent derailleur hanger is a frequent cause of poor shifting, particularly with index systems. Here's how to tell if your frame needs professional help.

1. Get behind the bike and sight along the bottom stretch of chain. The derailleur pulleys should be parallel with the chainrings and pointed straight ahead or slightly outward. If they're not, the rear derailleur hanger or rear frame triangle may be misaligned. If your bike shifts poorly after falling on its right side, a bent hanger is probably to blame.

2. Hold a ruler against the outer plate of the front derailleur cage. If it's not parallel to the chainrings, the derailleur or cage may need to be repositioned, or the seat tube may be misaligned. Uncorrectable front chain derailments are also an indication of seat tube misalignment.

■15 CHAIN CARE

A bicycle chain has more than 500 parts, all helping transmit your power to the rear wheel. With proper cleaning and lubrication, it will perform this task efficiently for thousands of miles. But if you neglect it and allow the chain to become dirty and dry, expect sluggish pedaling, poor shifting, and accelerated wear to teeth on the freewheel and chainrings.

There are almost as many theories about chain maintenance as there are chain parts. To find out what manufacturers recommend, we asked six of the biggest: Regina, Sedis, Shimano, SunTour, HKK, and Daido (DID). What follows is a compilation of their advice.

Quick Service

If you ride frequently, your chain should be lubricated weekly and after every rainy ride. Never allow the chain to become dry and squeaky.

Use a low-viscosity penetrating lubricant that doesn't leave a tacky film on the chain's surface. SunTour USA's technicians recommend Super Lube. HKK suggests Tri-Flow or WD-40. Daido favors WD-40. (SunTour also recommends hot paraffin baths; the others were unfamiliar with this method. See "Chain Care" in chapter 23.) Choose your lubricant and follow these steps.

1. Put the bike in a work stand or position it so the crank can be turned. Shift the chain to the smallest freewheel cog and largest chainring.

2. With your left hand, hold a rag (paper towels shred) around the chain between the rear derailleur and chainring. Use your right hand to turn the crank backward. After several revolutions, change to a clean part of the rag and continue turning.

3. Lightly spray lubricant on the portion of chain atop the freewheel cog as you slowly turn the crank backward several revolutions. Avoid excessive overspray. Next, position the spray nozzle above the chain where it engages the upper pulley of the rear derailleur. Spray the opposite side of the chain as you turn the crank.

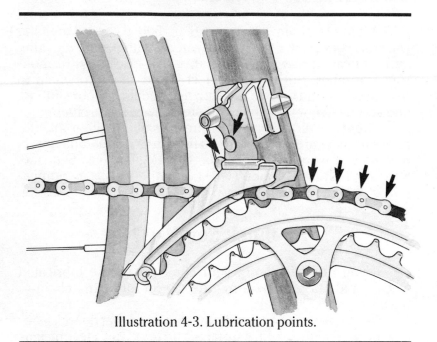

Illustration 4-3. Lubrication points.

4. Use a clean rag to wipe lubricant from the chain's surface, as in step 2. When you're finished, the chain should appear clean but not wet. Lubricant belongs inside the links, not outside where it gathers dust and dirt.

Full Service

When the chain is too dirty for on-bike cleaning, it must be degreased. Depending on your riding schedule and environment, this can be a weekly or monthly job. You need a chain rivet tool, a solvent such as kerosene or diesel (HKK recommends transmission fluid), rubber gloves, a paint tray, a toothbrush, some rags, newspaper to protect the floor, and a well-ventilated work area. (If you're using a Park or Vetta tool, degreasing is done with the chain on the bike. Follow the tool's directions.)

1. Using the chain tool, push any rivet until 80 percent of it protrudes through the side plate. Remove the tool and snap apart the chain by bending it away from the exposed pin. Shimano Uniglide chains require a special tool to prevent damage to the bulged side plates. Otherwise, use a standard tool and put the tip of a small screwdriver behind the bulged plate.

2. Measure the chain to see if it needs to be replaced rather than cleaned. Stretch it straight on a flat surface, and hold the end of a ruler to the center of any rivet. Then look at the 12-inch mark. On a new chain it will be at the center of a rivet. If this rivet is at 12⅛ inches or more, the chain is worn and should be discarded.

3. If the chain is usable, coil it flat in the pan. Cover with solvent and let it soak for 15 minutes. Occupy yourself by picking crud from between freewheel cogs with a small screwdriver. Put on rubber gloves, moisten the corner of a rag with solvent, and degrease everything the clean chain will touch (jockey wheels, freewheel teeth, chainring teeth, front derailleur cage).

4. With gloves still on, slosh the chain in the pan to allow solvent to flow through the links and loosen crud. Wear safety goggles in case it splashes.

5. With the chain submerged, scrub each link with the toothbrush. Then turn the chain and scrub the other side.

6. Pick up the chain by one end. Undo the kinks, use a clean rag to wipe it from top to bottom, then hang it to dry. Place a rag underneath to catch drips. Strain the solvent into an unbreakable container labeled "chain solvent," cap tightly, and store for future use or dispose of it in an ecological manner.

7. When the chain is "dry" (some solvents leave an oily film), reinstall it. Thread the chain through the front derailleur cage, over the smallest freewheel cog, and around the pulleys. Leave it off the chainring so you can easily snap the ends together. Then use the chain tool to push the rivet through, leaving equal amounts on either side of the link. *Note:* If you have a unidirectional chain (identified by asymmetrical side plates), orient it as it was before removal.

8. Bend the link to be certain it moves freely. If it binds, grasp the chain on either side and flex it laterally until it loosens.

9. Lubricate and wipe the chain as described under "Quick Service."

Chain Problems

Corrosion and poor quality are two common causes of recurring tight links that can cause skipping. Find them by watching the chain pass over the derailleur pulleys while pedaling backward by hand. Tight links won't flow smoothly. Loosen them with your chain tool or by bending them laterally with your hands. Lubrication will also help. Discard chains that have numerous tight links or are stiff with rust.

Troublesome or damaged links can be replaced. Be sure to use the identical width and brand. Drive out one pin on each side of the bad section, extract the links, and insert the new ones. Be sure to install the same number as were removed.

Rollers sometimes break, resulting in a crunching sound as they pass over the freewheel. To find a broken roller, inspect the chain from above while pedaling slowly by hand.

Carefully ride the bike after installing a new chain to see if it meshes with the cogs. Try each gear combination and note any skipping. Replace the worn cogs or the freewheel.

In general, next to keeping your tires properly inflated, cleaning and lubricating the chain is the best way to improve your bike's efficiency. It also prolongs the life of everything the chain touches.

16 FREEWHEEL COG REPLACEMENT

The chain and freewheel cogs wear together. Often, when you install a new chain, you'll discover that a cog or two must also be replaced. You'll know because the new chain will slip out of the teeth, creating noise and making the bike difficult to control. This problem is also likely to occur when a new freewheel is mated with an old chain.

There's no need to discard an entire $25 freewheel when a couple of $4 cogs are excessively worn. In fact, the body of a quality freewheel is capable of outlasting several generations of cogs.

By mastering a pair of simple tools called chainwhips (about $10 apiece at bike shops), you can easily replace worn cogs or tailor your freewheel to meet specific gearing needs.

The first step is to determine which cogs must be replaced. Install your new chain, then ride up a slight grade or drag your brakes to create plenty of pedaling resistance. For safety, remain seated and wear an approved helmet. If the chain slips you could lose control. Ride in all cogs and note where the chain skips.

The two smallest cogs are most likely to be excessively worn because they bear the greatest chain pressure per tooth. Your favorite cruising gear (the 17-tooth cog, for example) may also need replacing.

Removal

On most freewheels, the two or three smallest cogs screw (clockwise) onto the freewheel body. These cogs retain the others, which slide on.

Chainwhips are the only tools you'll need. Two are required— one to oppose the force you exert with the other. Chainwhips grip the cogs without damaging them, and the tools' long handles provide leverage for loosening or tightening. Remove the rear wheel from your bike and follow this procedure.

1. Stand with the wheel leaning against your legs, the freewheel away from you.

2. Wrap one chainwhip around the *largest* cog so its chain pulls clockwise on the teeth. Position the handle parallel to the floor. If you've done it right, the tool will hang in place.

3. Wrap the second chainwhip around the *smallest* cog so its chain pulls counterclockwise on the teeth. Position this handle opposite the other handle. (See illustration 4-4.)

4. Apply steady, downward pressure on both chainwhips

to unscrew the smallest cog. Apply Liquid Wrench or a similar penetrating lubricant if the cog doesn't budge. Don't increase leverage on the handle by using a pipe—excessive force may break something.

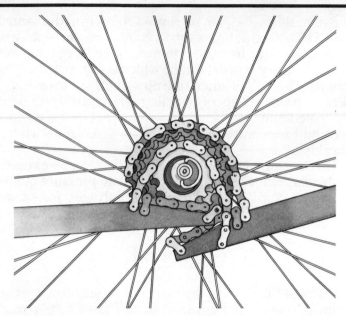

Illustration 4-4. Using chainwhips to remove freewheel cogs.

5. Unscrew the loosened cog by hand and lay it on your workbench, followed by any spacers you find. Place these parts in order of removal to avoid confusion during reassembly. Pay attention to cog orientation. Some cogs have distinct, but often unmarked, right and left sides. The cog's number of teeth may be stamped on the right (outward facing) side.

6. If the second cog unscrews with the first and you only need to replace one, screw them back into place and repeat steps 1 through 5 with a chainwhip on the second cog instead of the largest cog. Then use the same process to remove the second cog and any others that screw on.

Generally, all cogs come off the freewheel's right side. Regina's Oro and Extra freewheels are exceptions. These older models have threaded cogs, and the two largest screw counterclockwise onto the left side. Therefore, in step 4 of cog removal, you may inadvertently unscrew the largest cog rather than the smallest. To prevent this, move the chainwhip to the second- or third-largest cog. To remove the two remaining cogs after unscrewing those from the right side, you'll need to remove the body and take it to a shop that has a Regina freewheel vise.

Installation

While the cogs and spacers are off, clean them with a rag and kerosene, diesel, or a commercial solvent such as Simple Green. Make sure all threads are clean. Take worn cogs to the bike shop to buy exact replacements (or different sizes if you're customizing the gearing). Be certain which position each new cog is for. A 17-tooth for the third position, for example, may not fit the fourth position.

Now you can reassemble the freewheel. Grease the threads of screw-on cogs to make their removal easier next time. Uniformly tighten each one with a chainwhip before installing the next. This will prevent uneven tightening during use.

Finally, reinstall the rear wheel and take another test ride to make sure you've replaced all the defective cogs. One caution: Now that you've mastered chainwhips, you may start losing sleep over gear ratios.

Part Five
INTERNAL BEARINGS

■17■ CRANKSET OVERHAUL

Cranksets bear the full force of the pedal stroke and transfer your power to the chain. The crankset's bottom bracket bearings work best and last longest when they're clean, lubricated, and properly adjusted. If you ride a lot, you should overhaul the bottom bracket at least once a year. Mountain bikes and road bikes used in competition may need their bottom brackets overhauled more often.

Cranksets consist of a right and left crankarm, chainrings, and a bottom bracket assembly (this includes the axle, bearing cups, and bearings held inside the frame). The right crankarm has the chainrings attached to it. Quality bikes most often have cotterless cranks, and the instructions given here are for this type. Each cotterless crankarm has a square, tapered hole that fits onto the end of the axle, which is also square and tapered. The arm is press-fit into place with either a nut or a bolt, depending on the axle type.

The bottom bracket is housed within the frame's bottom bracket shell. A cup is threaded into each side of this shell. The cups and bearings support the axle and the crankarms attached to it, while allowing them to spin.

Sealed bottom brackets require little or no service because their bearings are protected from grit. In fact, some of these systems can only be serviced by the manufacturer. The ones that can be serviced at home require special (and expensive) tools. Consult your owner's manual or dealer to determine whether your bike has a sealed bottom bracket and, if so, how to obtain service instructions.

Disassembly

First, be sure you have all the tools and supplies necessary for the job. These include a chain removal tool, pedal wrench, crankarm wrench, crankarm extractor, adjustable cup tool, lockring tool, Allen wrenches, flat-head screwdriver, flashlight, solvent such as Simple Green, and an assortment of rags. You'll also need a tube of medium-weight lithium bicycle grease and new ball bearings or retainers of the appropriate number and size. If you don't know the latter, take a sample to a bike shop after you've dismantled the bottom bracket.

1. Remove the pedals from the crankarms, and remove the chain.

2. Remove the dust caps covering the crankarm fixing bolts. The wide slots are best turned with a quarter or a wide, flat-head screwdriver. Other caps accept Allen wrenches. (Some cranksets have one-step removal systems. In this case, simply unscrewing the Allen bolt brings the crankarm with it.)

3. Remove the bolt or nut that holds the crankarms on the axle. Use a crankarm wrench or thin-wall socket wrench. Some crankset manufacturers sell a handy tool, shown in illustration 5-1, that features a bolt wrench at one end, a crankarm extractor on the other, and wrench flats in between for gripping and turning the tool.

4. Pull the crankarms from the axle. (See illustration 5-1.) To use the extractor, first unscrew the center pin until it recedes. Then thread the tool all the way into the crankarm, and turn its center pin clockwise until it begins to push against the axle. Keep turning the pin until it forces the crankarm off the end of the axle.

5. Once the arms are removed, check the adjustment of the axle. Does it spin smoothly, or does it bind? Is it loose? How much dirt is clinging to the area around the axle? These are clues to the condition of the bottom bracket. Little or no roughness means a routine cleaning and replacement of the bearings is probably all that's necessary. Any looseness or clunking and grating sounds indicate some parts may need to be replaced. Wipe dirt from the bottom bracket area. This is also a good time to disassemble and clean the chainrings.

6. Use the lockring tool to unscrew (counterclockwise) the lockring from the adjustable cup on the left side of the

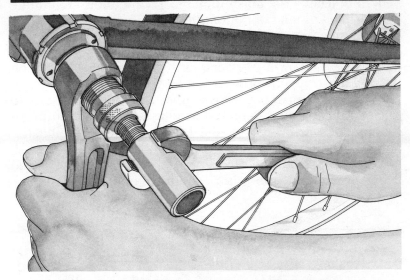

Illustration 5-1. Removing a crankarm with an extractor tool.

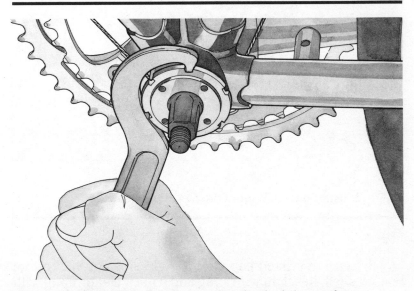

Illustration 5-2. Bottom bracket lockring tool.

bottom bracket. (See illustration 5-2.) Some tools are unique to a particular brand of bottom bracket, while others, such as hook spanners and pliers-type spanners, are more universal. Brand-specific tools are the surest fitting, but not all manufacturers have their own. Work cautiously because the threads on the ring and cup may produce metal slivers.

7. Place a rag or paper towel under the bottom bracket to catch errant bearings. Remove the adjustable cup by turning it counterclockwise with the adjustable cup tool. (See illustration 5-3.) Remove the axle, bearings, and dust sleeve. (Not all bottom brackets have a dust sleeve, which prevents dirt and debris in the frame tubes from contaminating the bearings.)

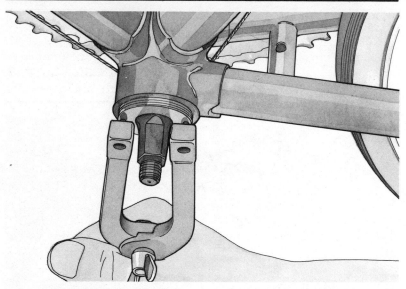

Illustration 5-3. Bottom bracket adjustable cup tool.

8. Leave the fixed cup (in the right side) of the bottom bracket shell. Reach in with a rag and wipe it clean, along with the inside of the shell. Clean all other bottom bracket components by soaking in solvent and scrubbing with a toothbrush. Dry them with compressed air or a clean rag.

9. Inspect the adjustable cup race for pitting or excessive wear on the bearing path. Check the axle, too. If a bearing retainer is used, check it for damage. Inspect the fixed cup with a flashlight. Replace any pitted or damaged components. Replace all the ball bearings, even if they don't appear worn. This is because load and wear distorts bearing shape. If the fixed cup is pitted and needs to be removed, you'll need a special tool or 12-inch adjustable wrench.

Reassembly

Once the bottom bracket parts have been removed, cleaned and/or replaced, you can reinstall the unit.

1. Apply a generous layer of grease to the fixed cup race, and install the ball bearings. If the bearings are in a retainer, pack it with grease and insert it into the cup. If the bearings are loose, place each bearing into the cup individually, relying on the grease to hold them until the axle is installed.

There is only one correct way to install a retainer in a cup. Therefore, it's important to remember the orientation during disassembly. The metal or plastic frame that holds the balls looks like a "C" in cross-section. In most cranksets, the open side of this "C" should face the shoulder of the axle. Thus, the open sides of the retainers will face each other when installed in the bottom bracket. Assembling the bottom bracket incorrectly precludes proper adjustment and can cause damage.

2. Insert the dust sleeve. If your bike doesn't have one, you may want to purchase one. Some mechanics like to apply a thin film of grease to the outside of the dust sleeve to capture grit. To retard corrosion, apply a thin film of grease to the surface of the axle, except for the tapers. Add a little extra at both bearing shoulders. Then take a close look at the axle. On most, one end is slightly longer than the other from the shoulder. Insert the longer end into the bottom bracket first so that it emerges through the fixed cup on the right (chainring) side of the bike.

3. Pack grease into the adjustable cup as you did the fixed cup, and install its set of bearings. Then screw it into the bottom bracket shell until you feel the bearings pressing snugly against the axle shoulders. Thread the lockring onto the adjustable cup and tighten it by hand.

4. Spin the axle to make sure the bearings are not binding. Try moving the axle up and down to check for looseness. If you need to alter the adjustment, unscrew the lockring a little and turn the adjustable cup until the axle spins smoothly, but without play. Once it's adjusted correctly, hold the adjustable cup stationary with its tool and firmly tighten the lockring.

5. Wipe all grease off the axle tapers and install the right crankarm. (Every major crankset manufacturer recommends that the axle tapers be free of lubricant. Grease can cause the arms to slide on too far.) Then grasp the crankarm at the end, and wiggle it. The extra leverage will allow you to detect even small amounts of play. Spin it a few times and wiggle it again. Eliminate any play with the methods described in step 4.

6. Place the other crankarm on the axle and screw on the nut or bolt. Tighten both sides snugly, but don't put all your weight behind it. If you have a torque wrench, tighten to 25 to 30 foot-pounds.

7. Finally, install the pedals, chain, and dust caps. You'll find it satisfying to know that the heart of your bike's drivetrain is working perfectly. Remember to retighten the crankarm bolts after 75 to 100 miles and check them periodically.

▪18 HUB OVERHAUL

Your bike will have one of three types of hubs—traditional ball and cone, labyrinth-sealed ball and cone, and those with cartridge-sealed bearings. The first two are easy to service; the last will be relatively easy or next to impossible for do-it-yourselfers, depending on its design. Consult your owner's manual or a local bike shop for advice.

Don't base your servicing schedule on mileage or time. Rather, remove the wheels from your bike monthly (twice a month for mountain bikes) and spin the hub axle between your thumb and forefinger. Assuming the hub cones are properly adjusted, the axles should turn freely without grinding or binding. If they turn too freely, the grease has probably washed out or dried up. In either case it's time to overhaul the hub.

Work Area

1. Spread out a clean rag to catch ball bearings. Better yet, work over a cafeteria tray.

2. Open a can or tube of hand cleaner and put a stack of paper towels nearby.

3. Pour an inch of solvent into an empty, wide-mouth jar. Simple Green is relatively safe and effective, but make sure there is plenty of ventilation and wear safety glasses.

4. Put at least three more clean rags and a couple of jar lids within easy reach.

5. If you're installing new bearings, unwrap them and segregate the smaller, front ones from the rear ones in separate jar lids. Most front hubs take ten $^3/_{16}$-inch balls per side, although some use nine $^7/_{32}$-inch balls. Virtually all rear hubs use nine ¼-inch balls per side.

6. You'll need a set of flat, open-end wrenches called cone wrenches (sizes 13-14mm and 15-16mm), a wide-blade screwdriver, a rubber or wooden mallet, and an expendable toothbrush.

7. Break out your favorite bicycle grease, but keep it contained until you're finished splashing solvent around.

Disassembly

1. Hang your bike from the rafters or secure it in a work stand. Remove the wheels.

2. Take off the freewheel. Shimano freehubs will remain in place until the axle cones are loosened.

3. Remove the axle nuts or quick-release skewers. (Screw the ends back onto the skewers to keep from losing parts.)

4. Place the rear wheel on your work area with its left side (as if you were sitting on the bike) facing up. With the appropriate cone wrenches, free the left-side locknut and remove it from the axle.

5. Slide off all washers. Sometimes keyed washers rotate and jam against the axle threads. If this happens, grab the offending washer with a pair of pliers and turn it (countering the axle's rotation with a cone wrench on the right-side cone) until the key returns to its groove. Then slide it off.

6. Unscrew the left-side cone and remove the axle from the underside. Be careful of ball bearings that may be clinging to the greasy axle or cones. Put all bearings in the solvent (if you are reusing them), along with the cone, locknut, washer(s) and right-side axle assembly. The freewheel cassette may come loose from Shimano freehubs at this point. If it does, simply slip it back on and proceed, mindful that it's unsecured.

7. Remove the rubber or metal dust cover on the hub shell's left side by gently levering it upward with a broad, flat screwdriver blade. Put the cover in the solvent. Scoop out the remaining left-side bearings and drop them into the solvent. Flip the wheel over and repeat this step. To contain runaway bearings, cup your hands over the hub shell openings as you flip the wheel.

Cleaning

1. Swish the soaking parts in the solvent.

2. Wipe out the hub shell and, with the corner of a clean rag that's been dipped in solvent, scrub the bearing races. When clean, wipe away the solvent with a dry corner of the rag.

3. One at a time, fish the cone, washer(s), locknut, and axle from the solvent and scrub them with a toothbrush. Rinse all pieces in the solvent and lay them to dry on a clean rag.

4. Remove the bearings and pour the used solvent into a coffee can for disposal. Buff the bearings with a clean rag and put them in a jar lid.

Inspection

1. Each ball bearing should gleam. Patches of dullness indicate wear. When in doubt, replace them. They're cheap, especially compared with other hub parts.

2. Each cone will sport a shiny ring that's been created by the bearings. Use a magnifying glass to look for "pits" (small potholes) in this polished path. Replace cones at the first sign of pitting. An uneven ball groove or a crack in the cone are also grounds for replacement. These problems will eventually deform the balls, which, in turn, will deform the bearing race in the hub shell—the most costly hub part to replace.

3. Inspect the bearing race for excessive wear, using the same criteria as with the cones. The races of high-quality hubs are worthy of replacement. Economy dictates that lesser hubs be replaced completely.

4. To facilitate reassembly, mark the position of the right-side cone with a felt-tip pen or piece of tape. Then remove the cone, washer(s) and locknut, and check the axle's straightness by rolling it on a flat surface. Slight axle deformity (about 0.5 mm) is not unusual. Anything more portends excessive wear or even axle failure.

Lubrication and Reassembly

1. Wash your hands with the cleaner and dry them thoroughly on a paper towel.

2. Lay a thin bead of hub grease around one bearing race. Smooth it with your finger.

3. Lay the cleaned or new ball bearings into the race, one at a time.

4. Lay another bead of grease over the balls. Smooth with your finger.

5. Insert the dust cover into the recess on the hub shell. If necessary, gently persuade it into place with a rubber or wooden mallet.

6. Carefully flip the wheel over and repeat steps 2–5. The dust cover and grease should hold the balls in place.

7. Screw the right-side cone, washer(s), and locknut onto the axle, making sure to align the cone with your mark. Tighten this assembly by using the cone wrenches to screw the cone and locknut toward each other.

8. Coat the face of the cone with a thin layer of grease, and insert the axle into the right side of the hub. On rear hubs the right side is threaded to accept freewheels, but on front hubs the sides are indistinguishable. Determine the rear wheel's right side first and observe which way the rim label faces. Then, orient the front rim to match.

9. Apply grease to the face of the left cone and screw it on until it's finger tight. Slide on the washer(s).

10. Use the cone wrenches to double-check the tightness of the *right-side* cone and locknut. The rotation of the wheel tends to loosen the right-side cone and draw it inward, damaging the hub if left unchecked. Therefore, the right side must be securely tightened before final adjustments are made to the left side.

11. Tighten the left-side locknut against the cone with the cone wrenches. Check the adjustment by alternately turning the axle between thumb and forefinger and rocking it sideways. The axle should turn freely and feel *slightly* loose (to allow for compression when the wheel is fastened to the frame).

When the wheel is installed, there should be no sideplay at the rim, and the weight of the valve stem (positioned at three or nine o'clock) should be enough to turn the wheel. Keep fussing until you get it right.

◼19◼ HEADSET OVERHAUL

It's easy to forget about the headset if it's working properly. But this important part of your bike should be overhauled once a year, more often if it's subjected to heavy use and grit. A neglected headset will eventually wear out pressed-in bearing races that require costly shop repair.

The headset components work together to support the fork in the frame while permitting it to rotate freely for steering. The headset must also withstand road shock. Rattles, clunks, grinding, or a notchy or stiff feel during steering are all symptoms of an overdue headset overhaul.

Conventional headsets use cups (the top one is adjustable) and cones (races) to retain the bearings. Two sets of bearings work together in a headset. Some headsets use cylindrical roller bearings rather than round ones.

Disassembly

For this procedure you'll need a wrench designed for your headset brand (don't use Channellock-type pliers, because they can cause damage); a 6mm Allen key to fit the handlebar stem bolt; a wooden or rubber mallet, or a hammer and block of scrap wood; new bearings to match those in your headset; solvent/cleaner; bike grease; and a few lint-free rags.

1. Remove the front wheel and detach the brake cable from the front calipers. Mark the handlebar stem position with tape where it meets the headset.

2. Loosen the bolt at the top of the handlebar stem. Unscrew it until its head is just above the stem, then tap it down with the mallet (or cover the bolt with the block of wood and use the hammer). This frees the plug that secures the stem inside the fork steerer tube. Remove the bar and stem, and hook them over the top tube.

3. Unscrew the headset locknut using the special headset wrench. (See illustration 5-4.) Remove the remaining parts and place them in sequence on your work table so you'll remember their order. If there's a second locknut, remove it as well. Lift off the notched lockwasher and the reflector bracket or brake hanger if there is one.

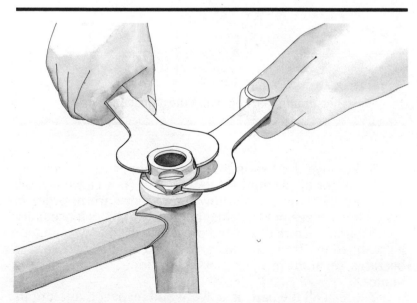

Illustration 5-4. Using headset wrenches to unscrew the locknut.

4. Unscrew the top (adjustable) cup. While doing this, support the fork from below with one hand. (See illustration 5-5.) This prevents the lower bearings from falling out. Watch for loose bearings as you unscrew the adjustable cup. Caged bearings are commonly used and make the job easier. Note that the open side of the cage's "C" shape faces the race.

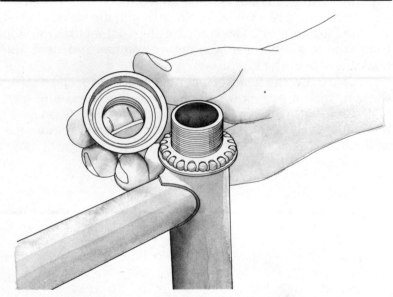

Illustration 5-5. Removing the adjustable cup.

5. Remove the bearings from the upper head race and save them for inspection. If they're loose (not caged), you'll also need to know exactly how many there are in order to match the replacements. A magnet easily gathers loose balls.

6. Slide the fork down and out of the frame, watching for loose bearings from the lower cup. Keep the two sets of bearings separate in case they're not identical in size and number.

7. Clean all the parts in solvent and inspect them for pits and cracks. Replace as necessary. Replacing the press-fit fork crown race, the lower head cup, or the upper head race requires special tools. Since they cost about $140, have a shop do it, then continue with the next step.

Reassembly

1. Clean the steerer tube with a rag, then coat it from the top (including threads) to the fork crown race with a film of grease. This prevents corrosion. Also, pack grease into the lower head cup, the adjustable cup, and the upper head race.

2. Install the bearings in the lower cup. Place the fork in the frame, being careful not to pinch the rubber seal (if there is one).

3. Install the bearings in the upper race. Then thread the adjustable cup and turn it until it contacts the bearings. Don't try to adjust the bearing tension yet.

4. Replace the reflector bracket or brake hanger (if any), lockwasher, locknut—whatever was taken off—in the correct order. But don't tighten the locknut.

5. Tighten the stem bolt just enough to catch the plug in the bottom of the stem, then replace the stem in the steerer tube. Match its original height with the tape, then tighten.

6. Adjust the headset bearings. Hand-tighten the adjustable cup until it contacts the bearings, then back off between one-eighth and one-quarter turn. Tighten the locknut. Check for correct adjustment by alternately pushing and pulling on the fork and handlebar. Turn the bar and do this at several different locations. If there's any play, loosen the locknut, tighten the adjustable cup a bit more, then retighten the locknut and try again. Turn the bar to detect any resistance. Binding indicates the bearings are too tight. It will take a few tries to adjust this exactly. Work from loose to just right. Be careful because overtightening can ruin the headset.

7. Replace the front wheel. Loosen the stem bolt, align the stem with the wheel, then snug the bolt. (Not too tight—it must be able to pivot in the steerer tube during a crash to reduce the chance of parts breakage and personal injury.) Finally, reattach and adjust the brake cable.

█20█ PEDAL OVERHAUL

Inexpensive pedals may not be worth the time and trouble to service. They'll usually work well for several years without any attention, then they can be replaced when they begin to have problems.

A good pair of pedals, however, deserves the kind of care given to cranksets, hubs, and headsets. Regular maintenance will ensure efficient, reliable performance and long life.

Since pedals protrude from the bike and are near the ground, they're vulnerable to collisions with various objects. Often the damage is only cosmetic, but sometimes the cage and/or axle may be bent or broken, making the pedal dangerous to use.

Depending on the model, the pedal's cage and other parts may be replaceable. If this is the case, it's best to try to repair the pedal instead of buying a new one, especially since pedals are usually available only in pairs.

Disassembly

1. Pedals should be removed from the bike for servicing. Just keep in mind that a left pedal has backward threads—to unscrew it from the crankarm you turn it clockwise. The right pedal has normal threads.

2. Remove the dust cap to expose the axle and bearing assembly. Some dust caps are pried out with a small, flat-head screwdriver, while others unscrew. Under the dust cap you'll see a locknut on the end of the axle, a lockwasher, a cone, and the bearings.

3. Use a bench vise or wrench to hold the opposite end of the axle, then unscrew the locknut counterclockwise. Slide off the lockwasher, then unscrew the cone, exposing the bearings.

4. Holding the axle in place from the opposite end, tip over the pedal and shake the bearings onto a rag. Count them and record the number. Then do the same for the bearings on the other side by pulling out the axle. This may take some effort if there is a rubber seal.

5. Wipe all parts clean with a rag. Use a solvent if necessary, but keep it away from plastic, rubber, and leather. Get out all the old grease and traces of solvent. Inspect the axle, cone, and bearing races. If there is pitting or other damage, check with your bike shop about replacement parts. Buy new ball bearings.

Reassembly

1. Pack medium-weight grease into the pedal's inner and outer bearing races. Lay in the same number of balls that came out. If you're confused, the correct number is a full race minus one. Coat the axle with grease and push it through the pedal body until its cone seats against the bearings.

2. Turn over the pedal and screw on the cone with your fingers until it contacts the bearings. Put on the lockwasher, then the locknut.

3. As in all bearing adjustments, it's a matter of trial and error to correctly tighten the axle assembly. Using the tip of your small screwdriver, play with the cone's position until almost all play is out of the axle. Then hold the cone still and tighten the locknut against it.

4. Spin the axle. If it binds or is loose when you wiggle it, loosen the locknut and readjust the cone. It's right when the axle spins smoothly but isn't loose. Make sure the locknut is tight, then replace the dust cap.

5. Before screwing the pedal into its crankarm, coat its threads with grease. Be careful not to crossthread. Use a wrench to make it snug.

Part Six

MOUNTAIN BIKE MAINTENANCE

▪21 CARE AND CLEANING

After paying all that cash for a beautiful, new, smooth-running mountain bike, you may be reluctant to head for the mud pits and dusty trails. Don't be. Although Mother Earth can make your 5-hour-old ATB look like it has suddenly suffered five years of deterioration, the dirt won't hurt as long as you take the necessary precautions.

Our experts—one from Vermont and the other from California—have had years of experience riding and maintaining off-road bikes. Don Cuerdon's the muck expert, having developed his ATB skills in the lush and muddy Northeast. Gary Fisher, the owner of Fisher MountainBikes, helped pioneer off-road cycling on the arid, dusty roads of Marin County's Mt. Tamalpais. Together, they've seen (and cleaned) it all.

What follows are their best tricks to help you keep your mountain bike working well and avoid premature parts replacement. Much of this maintenance can be done in just a few minutes.

Cleaning

The most important rule in ATB maintenance is to clean the bike frequently. Dirt acts as a grinding compound when it gets between moving parts, so the sooner you remove it, the better. In muddy or sandy conditions you may have to clean the bike after every ride.

If you're careful, you can use a car wash. Just don't let the high-pressure wand blast water into the bearings. Almost all mountain bikes have sealed bearings in the hubs and crank, but no seals are impermeable. And while we're on the subject, never ride with the crank completely submerged. The flexing from pedaling will let water through the seals. Splashing through a creek is fine; riding downstream with a snorkel isn't.

The European method of bike washing works best. You'll need a bucket of hot water, a mild detergent such as Bike Wash, three nylon-bristle brushes, a high-viscosity degreaser such as Gunk, a small screwdriver, a rinse bucket or garden hose, and an old towel. Use a floor brush for the big parts of the bike, a bottle brush for the nooks and crannies, and another bottle brush designated for greasy parts. Now move the car out of the driveway and let's get to work.

1. Initial rinse. Remove the major muck by gently spraying with the garden hose or dousing the bike with a bucketful of water. Never wipe dirt or mud from your bike with a rag—it will scratch the finish.

2. Degrease. Remove the wheels. Brush degreaser onto the derailleurs, chain, and chainrings. Mush it between the freewheel cogs. You must use a high-viscosity degreaser so it doesn't run inside sealed bearings. The thick stuff also removes surface grime from the chain without washing anything into the pins and rollers (which could cause more wear than leaving the chain dirty). Avoid aerosol degreasers—they're too light.

3. Rinse. Use water and the greasy brush to rinse the chain, derailleurs, and chainrings. A small screwdriver is handy for picking the loosened crud out of the freewheel.

4. Wheels. Start with the hub, using the clean bottle brush and a bucket of soapy water. Continue cleaning outward until you reach the rim. Scrub the rim and tire with the floor brush. Rinse.

5. Frame. Use the floor brush, then the clean bottle brush to get behind the chainrings and other hard-to-reach spots. Don't forget under the saddle. Rinse and then install the wheels.

6. Dry. Wipe off water with a towel, then put the bike in a warm place to dry thoroughly. The tubes of better mountain bikes have drain holes to let moisture out and allow dry air to get in.

Inspection

It's easier to inspect for damage and other problems when a bike is clean. Here's the checklist.

1. Frame. Soon after you buy your mountain bike, measure its wheelbase (the distance from the rear axle to the front axle when the front wheel is straight ahead). Remeasure each time you inspect the bike. If the wheelbase grows or shrinks, something's damaged. Also look for cracks in the lugs or frame joints. These may appear as paint cracks. Inspect the tubes for bulges, dents, or ripples. If something looks suspicious, see a professional.

2. Wheels. Spin the wheels. Watch between the brake pads for dents, bulges, wobbles, and the like in the rims. Look for loose or broken spokes. Check the tires for cuts, bulges, and embedded debris. When the wheels are removed for washing, turn the axles with your fingers. Any roughness indicates the need for cone adjustment or repacking. Look for broken or bent freewheel teeth.

3. Handlebar grips. Twist them. If they move, remove them and apply rubber cement. Use enough so they slip on easily. You'll need a stickier glue such as 3M Fast Tack Trim Adhesive for soft foam grips.

4. Chain. Count 24 links and measure from the first pin to the last. A new chain should measure 12 inches. If yours is 12⅛ inches or more, replace it. Riding with a worn chain accelerates wear to chainrings and freewheel cogs. It also impairs shifting performance.

5. Derailleur alignment. This is especially critical with an index system. Sighting from behind the bike, the pulleys should be aligned vertically and parallel to the plane of the chainrings and freewheel. Anything crooked should be straightened by your dealer.

6. Brakes. Inspect the pads for wear and embedded debris. Check for frayed cables. Replace anything that is even remotely suspect. You must have reliable brakes in the outback.

7. Pedals. Occasionally remove them from the crankarms and turn the axles with your fingers, feeling for roughness or excessive play. Then look closely for fractures in the pedal body and cage. Ditto for the toe clips, if you use them. Make sure their bolts are tight.

8. Bottom bracket. With the pedals off, drape the chain around the bottom bracket shell so it doesn't touch the chainrings. Place your ear against the saddle and turn the cranks. Anything funny going on inside the bottom bracket will be amplified through the frame and become audible at the saddle. If you're not sure you like what you hear, remove the crankarms and turn the axle with your fingers to check the adjustment.

9. Headset. Grasp the top tube behind the head tube, lift the front wheel a couple of inches, and nudge the handlebar so it turns gently from side to side. If it wants to catch in the straight-ahead position, the headset is damaged. If it locks like it has auto pilot, it's ruined. The best solution for this is prevention—frequent checks to make sure the headset is properly adjusted. A loose one will clunk when you squeeze the front brake hard and rock the bike back and forth. A tight one won't let the front end pivot fully when you pick it up and nudge the handlebar. One way to get more miles from a damaged headset is to install loose ball bearings in place of the retainers. Additional bearings will fit in each race, so they won't sit in the dents that are causing the catch. You can also have the shop partially rotate the headset cups.

Lubrication

When your bike is dry, lubricate the parts you degreased and any others that may need it.

1. Chain, derailleur pulleys, rollercam brakes. The lubricant must correspond to the environment. In dry weather, use a product with a volatile carrier that penetrates well, then evaporates, leaving a viscous lubricant in place. Tri-Flow and Sta-Lube are good choices. Use a rag to protect the rear rim from overspray, and wipe away excess lubrication. Lube the exposed moving parts of a rollercam brake.

For wet weather or muddy terrain, a sticky oil works best. Try Campagnolo and Phil Wood. Although they collect dirt, they prevent anything raunchy from seeping into the chain's pins and rollers and the derailleur's pulley bushings. European cyclocross racers sometimes coat their chains with grease when the course is extra muddy. The grease simply displaces the mud.

Paraffin isn't a good choice for mountain bike chains if you usually ride in wet, muddy conditions. The wax won't last long enough, so the chain will have to be removed and rewaxed too often. In drier climates, paraffin works well because it doesn't attract dust and sand.

2. Seatpost. If you use your mountain bike correctly, you'll frequently change your seat height. Lowering the saddle is necessary for good control on descents, so the seatpost/seat tube must be kept clean and lubricated. Remember to mark the post before you pull it from the frame in order to retain your correct saddle height. If you use a Hite-Rite seat locator, put a piece of masking tape just above the Hite-Rite sleeve. Loosen the sleeve and pull the post from the frame. Wrap a rag around a screwdriver and clean the seat tube. Lubricate the seatpost with your Campy or Phil oil and reassemble the Hite-Rite.

3. Cables. Free-sliding derailleur cables are always desirable, and they're mandatory with index shifting. Grease gets too dirty and creates drag in the system. Shimano recommends running its derailleur cables dry. If this doesn't suit you, try pure silicone spray. Braking performance can be improved by lubricating the cable end buttons at the levers.

4. Sealed bearings. Sealed bearings can and should be serviced. Carefully remove the seal with an X-Acto knife or similar tool. Be careful not to dent the seal's seat. Thorough cleaning of the internal parts is crucial because new grease will be degraded by the old. Use a solvent such as kerosene or a degreaser and water. Wear safety goggles. Avoid getting solvent on the tires or any other rubber parts. Flush thoroughly and dry with compressed air (available by the can at photography stores).

Repack the bearings with high-viscosity grease. Fisher MountainBikes come packed with Sta-Lube Boat Trailer Wheel Bearing Grease. Gary likes it so much he supplies it to the factory in Japan. (It's a bit too gooey for road bikes, however.)

5. Saddle. Water and dirt can turn your saddle's supple leather covering into something akin to sandpaper. Preserve the leather by rubbing in Brooks Proofhide or Nivea skin cream. Dust the surface with baby powder or talc to make it slippery again.

6. Pump. Avoid pump failures by keeping the gasket

lubed. Use petroleum jelly on leather gaskets and K-Y Jelly on rubber ones.

For mountain bike repair procedures, see the other chapters in this book. Most of the steps are the same for road and off-road components.

Finally, remember that you've got to get your mountain bike filthy in order to take care of it right. Happy (muddy and dusty) trails!

Part Seven

DETAILING

22 FRAME PAINT TOUCH-UP

We convinced Peter Weigle, master framebuilder and restorer, to share some of the paint repair tricks he has learned. Says Weigle, "There are two absolutes in frame touch-up. You absolutely must cover bare metal spots to protect the frame's integrity, and the repair absolutely never looks as good as new." With this in mind, here's how to get the best possible results as you try to cure what's called "cancer of the tubes."

Cosmetic Surgery

"It's difficult to get an exact match of the original paint," claims Weigle. "Even original paint will appear lighter or darker when brushed on rather than sprayed." One trick, he says, is to peruse the model paint display at a neighborhood hobby shop and purchase the closest color you can find. If you're artistically adept, try mixing colors to get a more exact match.

For repairing a fresh, small nick or gouge, follow these steps.

1. Clean the area to be painted with rubbing alcohol and allow to dry for 10 minutes.

2. Position the bike with the nick facing up.

3. Use a toothpick, the fuzzy end of a cardboard match, or a tiny brush to carefully apply paint to the flaw. Be careful not to get any on the edges of the crack.

4. If necessary, repeat steps 1 through 3 on successive days until the nick is evenly filled with paint.

5. Let the paint cure for two weeks. Then rub the spot with fine compound and a soft cloth. Finish the job with a quality auto or bike wax such as Bike Elixir or Dave Moulton's Frame Wax.

Large chips and scratches require more work. Follow these steps for troublesome areas.

1. Feather the edges of the chip by wet-sanding with 600-grit paper. Don't remove any more paint than necessary.

2. Clean the area with rubbing alcohol.

3. Paint the chip with a brush that's sized for the job.

4. Wet-sand and repaint each day until you achieve the desired result.

5. After two weeks of curing, compound and wax the spot.

If your attempt at repair looks worse than the original flaw, consider some strategic camouflage.

1. Many component companies offer tastefully designed decals that can cover poor repairs.

2. Wrap contrasting or complementary colored plastic tape around tubing to hide damage. A strip around the down and top tube where the front brake and handlebar make contact will prevent chipping.

3. If your right chainstay is a problem area, cover it with a commercial slap panel. This will prevent future nicks and chips caused by a bouncing chain.

Temporary Bypass

If you intend to have your frame professionally painted at season's end, you need only inhibit corrosion until then. And if your bike fits well and performs to your liking, it's well worth the $100 to $200 it costs to have it refurbished. As Weigle says, "Nothing's more satisfying than the look on a customer's face when he first sees his old friend reborn."

For temporary repairs:

1. Remove rust by carefully sanding and scrubbing with a tiny wire brush. Pay attention to top tube cable guides, the area under the rear brake cable and around the lugs, fork crown, and bottom bracket.

2. When all traces of corrosion are gone, clean the bare metal with rubbing alcohol.

3. Cover the bare spots by brushing on a rust-inhibiting primer such as Rustoleum.

4. Get your frame to the refinisher as soon as the season's over. October to April is their busy season.

An Ounce of Prevention

Weigle "undercoats" all his framesets with a Cosmoline-like, industrial, anticorrosion compound. He applies it on the unpainted inside surface of the tubing. "It's never too late to start," says Weigle. Here's how to do it yourself.

1. Remove all components from the frame, including headset races and bottom bracket cups.

2. Spray liberal amounts of anticorrosion compound into every accessible tube. LPS-3 is a good choice. However, it needs to be reapplied more often than greasier or waxier substances. At *Bicycling,* we use Care Clear Corrosion Prevention Compound. It comes with a tiny hose and nozzle designed for spraying into drying holes in seatstays and fork blades.

3. Turn the frame several times during application to ensure complete coverage.

4. Allow the fluid to dry, dribble out, or coagulate before reassembly.

Routine Care

Keep the outside of your frameset safe from oxidation by waxing it at least once a month. If you don't have the time or patience to give it a high-quality waxing, a weekly rubdown with spray furniture polish is better than nothing. As always, pay special attention to potential trouble spots, and do the following.

1. Use a soft toothbrush to work wax into fork crown cut-out details and cable guides. Sweat tends to pool in these areas and accelerate corrosion.

2. "Keep chrome clean and waxed from day one because there's no hope once it begins to pit," says Weigle. Chrome brighteners or cleaners from an automotive store work well. Finish the job by waxing as you would painted sections.

Those who own carbon fiber and aluminum frames are spared from these preventive and restorative chores. But for those of us still riding the ferrous sure-bet, a little care will prevent cancer of the tubes.

23 WEATHERPROOFING

Riding in wet, dirty conditions can undo careful maintenance work. Grit fouls the chain first, then works its way into the hubs, headset, and bottom bracket. Moisture can rust steel frame tubes inside and out. Here are some easy, inexpensive ways to prevent weather-induced damage.

Frame Protection

1. Repair frame nicks and scratches with touch-up paint, available at bike shops, hobby shops, or auto parts stores. (See chapter 22 for pointers.)

2. After all bare metal has been covered, clean and wax the frame. Wax protects the finish against fine scratches and prevents rust. Car wax is acceptable, though framebuilders recommend using a soft, nonabrasive substance such as Bike Elixir Cleaner/Protector or Dave Moulton's Frame Wax, especially for frames painted with lacquer. Du Pont Imron does not need to be waxed, but a mild wash and wax will enhance its finish.

3. Whenever you overhaul a crankset or headset, or remove the seatpost, spray the inside of all accessible tubes with an anticorrosion solution such as LPS-3, available at hardware or auto supply stores. Oil may be used, but it tends to flow to the bottom of the frame and evaporate.

4. If your bike is exposed to salt and moisture, whether from ocean breezes, winter road crews, or sweat, a lightweight lubricant such as WD-40 will help prevent corrosion if applied lightly to the outside of the frame. For indoor trainer workouts, also drape a towel over the top tube.

5. If you do a lot of riding in inclement weather, fenders will protect your body and bike frame, plus save on clean-up time and maintenance. Use full-size fenders—the more they cover, the better.

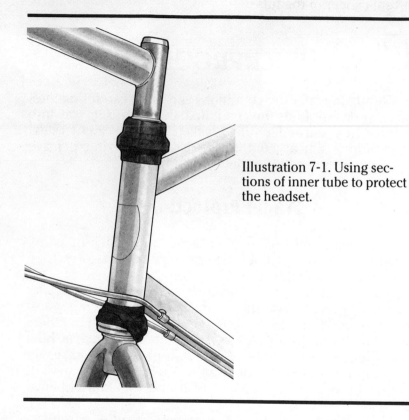

Illustration 7-1. Using sections of inner tube to protect the headset.

Chain Care

For extremely wet conditions, some experienced mountain bikers rely on heavy oil, such as a foaming motorcycle chain lube, to repel water. Some road race team mechanics wipe a thin layer of white lithium grease over the lubed chain to keep moisture out.

Paraffin treatment is another alternative. It's dry, so it doesn't hold grit. Here's how to do it.

1. Use solvent to remove all oil and grease from the chain and drivetrain. Let the components dry.

2. Soak the chain in a can of melted paraffin for at least 10 minutes. Hot paraffin (300°F) penetrates best, but keep it away from open flame and heating coils—paraffin is flammable. A "Fry Daddy" or other electric deep fryer, placed outdoors where it can be watched, is handy for this procedure.

3. Remove and hang the chain so the hot wax can drip off. Allow the chain to cool and then reinstall it. With your bike on a repair stand, spin through the gears to loosen the links and allow excess wax to flake off.

4. Repeat this procedure every 300 miles or when the chain becomes dirty. There is no need to use solvent for subsequent cleanings because the hot wax will flush away the grit.

Bearings

To withstand muddy, wet riding conditions, pack your hub, pedal, bottom bracket, and headset bearings in heavy, water-resistant grease such as Super Lube or Campagnolo's 02-ZPT. Some mountain bike enthusiasts prefer boat trailer wheel bearing grease, which is waterproof and available at marine stores.

Headset bearings can be protected with seals made from old inner tubes. It's convenient to install these when overhauling your headset. (See chapter 19.) When the headset is apart, 2-inch sections of old inner tube are placed over the top and bottom of the head tube. When the headset is rebuilt, the sections are pulled over the cups to seal out water and grit. They can be snipped off when no longer needed.

Rubber ring seals known as "O-rings" are available from hardware stores and can be used in a number of places to seal out water and grit. For instance:

- Above or within the outermost headset locknut.
- Over the bottom bracket axle, against the fixed cup

and adjustable cup. Use several on each side so the innermost rings stay snug against the cups.
- Over the hub locknuts, against the dust caps.
- Over the pedal axle, against the pedal cage.

Other Tricks

- Remove and degrease derailleur and brake cables that run underneath the bottom bracket, then lubricate by running them through a cake of paraffin. The paraffin will not attract road sludge.
- Use Armor-All to keep rubber brake lever hoods from drying and cracking.
- If your bike gets immersed in water or caught in a downpour, removing the seatpost and the bottom bracket will allow the moisture in the frame to evaporate quickly, minimizing damage. Placing the frame in a warm place or in the sun will also speed evaporation.

24 PERSONAL ADJUSTMENTS

While many cyclists look toward saddle height and frame dimensions when trying to alleviate discomfort, the solution may be at their fingertips. Problems such as back pain, hand numbness, and upper-body fatigue can result from an improperly positioned handlebar, stem, or levers.

The fit of these parts can be varied several ways. Road bike bars come in different widths and drop sizes, stems vary in extension, and brake levers can be moved vertically on the bar. Mountain bike bars are available with different bends (from nearly straight for fast riding to upright for use on easy trails or pavement), stems have various rise angles and extensions, and the brake levers and shifters can be rotated for optimum wrist position.

Road Bikes

Stems. To raise or lower your stem, loosen the center bolt three or four turns with a 5 or 6mm Allen wrench and tap it with a rubber or wooden mallet. This will free the expander that holds the stem in the steerer tube.

A stem that's set too high may break or damage the threaded portion of the steerer tube. Most stems have marks that indicate maximum height. Keep at least 2½ inches buried.

Overtightening the stem may cause the steerer tube to bulge. Hence, tighten it just enough to keep it from slipping during normal use. Test tightness by holding the front wheel between your legs and striking the handlebar. It shouldn't pivot. If it does, continue tightening and testing until it doesn't. If additional leverage is needed, grip the Allen wrench with an adjustable wrench.

Keep in mind that handlebars have different diameters. To ensure a tight fit, use the same brand of bar and stem.

To determine proper stem extension you must first establish your correct fore/aft saddle position. When the crankarms are horizontal, the bony protrusion just below your forward kneecap should be directly over the pedal axle. Use a plumb line to check this.

When stem extension is correct, your back should be straight. This position facilitates breathing and a relaxed upper body. Too short an extension causes the back to arch, compressing the diaphragm. Conversely, too long an extension results in locked elbows, arm fatigue, and back strain. Frequent movement on the seat is one indication of improper extension. Long stems make you slide forward to reach the bar, while short stems require moving to the rear to breathe easier and stretch your back.

Here are two other methods for determining proper stem extension.

- When riding on level ground with your hands on the brake lever hoods and elbows bent, the handlebar should obscure the front hub.
- With your hands on the drops and your forearms

horizontal to the road, your knees should overlap your elbows at the top of the pedal stroke.

Stems are available with extensions from 5 to 14 centimeters (measured from the center of the bolt to the center of the bar).

To determine optimum stem height, place a yardstick or straightedge on the saddle so that it extends over the stem. When the saddle is level, the top of the stem should be 1 to 3 inches below the straightedge.

Riders with long arms or torsos can lower the stem for comfort and aerodynamics. Conversely, cyclists with short upper-body dimensions or back problems can raise the stem so it's level with the seat. This is the position many tourists favor. However, don't raise the stem above seat level because this puts too much weight on the saddle and can cause soreness.

Handlebars. A bar that's too narrow compresses your chest and restricts breathing, while a bar that's too wide makes you less aerodynamic. Generally, your handlebar should be as wide as your shoulders. Most bars are available in 2-centimeter increments, from 38- to 46-centimeter widths (measured center to center). Women typically use a 38- or 40-centimeter bar, while men use 40 or 42 centimeters.

The depth of the drops is determined by the size of your hands. (Bigger hands require a deeper drop.) Measure drop from the center of the lower, straight portion of the bar to the center of the uppermost section—as if measuring the diameter of a circle. A drop of less than 14 centimeters is considered shallow, 14 to 15 centimeters is medium, and more than 15 centimeters is deep. The Fit Kit bicycle sizing system (used by many bike shops) has a device for measuring hand size. If your shop does not have the system, try this: Close your hand around a tube that's roughly the same diameter as your handlebar (a thick felt-tip marker will do). Then put your fist on a flat surface so that the tube is perpendicular to it. Measure the height of your fist in this position. If it's 2¾ inches or less you need a shallow drop; 2¾ to 3½ inches requires a medium drop; and 3½ inches or more requires a deep drop. Also, when riding on the drops your forearms should easily clear the bend of the bar above your hand. A bar that's too shallow may rub against your forearms when you stand to sprint.

The angle of the handlebar is also important. Generally,

it's correct when the bottom, flat section is parallel to the frame's top tube. But some riders prefer to rotate the bar so that this section is angled down toward the rear slightly. This facilitates resting atop the brake lever hoods. The angle shouldn't exceed 10 degrees, however, or it'll become difficult to reach the bottom of the brake levers when riding on the drops.

Brake levers. Use a straightedge to determine correct brake lever position. (See illustration 7-2.) Start by loosening the lever clamps enough to allow slight movement. (Unscrew the bolt inside each lever body two or three turns.) Hold the straightedge under the flat portion of the drops so it extends forward. Then position each lever so its tip just touches the straightedge. (If a lot of movement is required, you may need to remove and rewrap the handlebar tape.) Be sure the levers are facing straight forward before tightening the clamps.

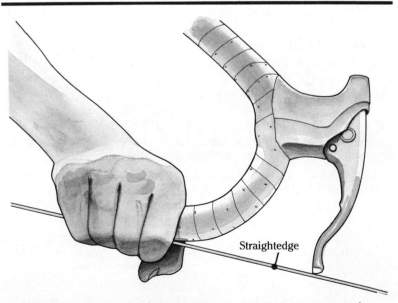

Straightedge

Illustration 7-2. Determining brake lever position on a road bike.

Riders with small hands may need "junior" or adjustable levers. Shallow- or medium-drop bars are required with these. When positioning such levers on a medium-drop bar, leave a half-inch gap between the lever tip and the straightedge. The tips should contact the straightedge when using a shallow-drop bar.

Shift levers. Most road bike shifters mount to braze-ons, and their position cannot be changed. Bikes requiring down tube clamps often have a stop brazed underneath to prevent slippage. Position the shifter clamp against this. If there is no stop, place the clamp so the tip of each lever is 1 to 2 inches from the head tube.

Some riders like to loosen the front derailleur cable so that derailleur action begins with the lever pulled back slightly from the down tube. This makes it easier to grasp the lever when shifting to the large chainring.

Mountain Bikes

Stems. The same general procedures for tightening and installing stems discussed at the beginning of the road bike section apply. Use a plumb line to determine proper stem rise angle (the angle formed by the vertical part of the stem and the extension). The line should fall from the tip of your nose to the handlebar when you are in your normal riding position. (Pedal backward to be sure you're seated comfortably, and bend your elbows slightly.) The optimum stem will position your back 45 degrees to the ground. A friend can help with this, or you can place a stationary trainer beside a mirror.

Many riders use a high-rise stem (and bar) in the hope it will alleviate back or neck pain. Unfortunately, this often aggravates the problem, as more road shock is transmitted to the small of the back when so much weight is over the rear wheel. It also reduces pedaling power. Only when leaning forward do you fully use the strong muscles in your lower back and buttocks.

Compared to road models, mountain bike stems don't have much vertical adjustability. When changing stem height, keep in mind that most also support the front brake cable housing. Hence, moving your stem vertically changes the front brake adjustment. (Lowering the stem loosens it; raising the stem tightens it.) Unless you loosen the cable anchor, you'll be unable to raise the stem significantly. Once you find the best position, mark it with a piece of colored tape for future reference. If you raise and lower the stem often, consider using a headset cable stop to avoid brake adjustment problems.

Handlebars. There are two types of mountain bike handlebars. The most common, called a "flat" bar, has a slight bend but no rise. Such a bar lies flat when placed on a table. The second type, called an "upturned" bar, resembles those found on old newspaperboy bikes and has a slight rise resulting in a more upright position. This kind of bar cannot be laid flat.

With either, use a position that feels natural for your wrists. Bending your wrists up, down, or sideways to grasp the bar will result in soreness or injury, especially in rough terrain. Generally, upturned bars should be positioned so the rising portion is angled slightly back toward the rider.

A flat bar can be positioned many different ways depending on terrain and riding style. While off the bike, extend your arms in front of you at normal riding width and make a fist with each hand. Notice that the tunnel through your fingers forms an angle. Use the bend to accommodate this natural wrist inclination. The most common position is with the bend turned toward the rider and tipped up slightly.

The width of most current mountain bike bars varies from 21 to 24 inches (measured end to end). Generally, a wider bar gives better slow-speed control, while a narrower bar affords a more aerodynamic position for fast riding. It's possible to make your bar narrower by cutting it with a hacksaw. Before doing this, however, you may wish to test the narrower width by moving the grips and levers inward.

When bar position is changed or when a new bar is installed, recheck your riding position in the mirror or with the plumb line method.

Brake levers. Mountain bike brake levers are available for different hand sizes. There are also adjustable models that change the range of lever travel so it starts closer to the hand grip.

To find the best lever position, start by loosening the levers enough so they can be moved. While in the saddle, place the levers at an angle that doesn't require bending your wrists up or down. Bent wrists hinder braking ability, and a severe bump could make you lose your grip.

The lever tips shouldn't extend beyond the end of the handlebar, because they'll be damaged if the bike falls over.

Shift levers. Most mountain bike shift levers mount atop the bar. Like brake levers, they should be placed at an angle that doesn't require bending your wrist. This is accomplished by rotating the shift levers so their movement parallels that of the brake levers.

In addition, the shifters should not overlap the grips, since this will cause them to rub against your hands in certain gears.

Shift levers that mount under the bar became available in 1990. This is a welcome innovation, since the surest grip comes when your thumb is under the handlebar.

Part Eight
SPECIAL
OCCASIONS

▪25 SPRING TUNE-UP

You may be ready to begin the new cycling season, but can your bike say the same? As soon as you remember where you left it last fall—attic? windtrainer? roof of the car?—haul it into your workshop for an important preseason inspection and tune-up.

Go through the following checklist with your bike in a work stand, hanging from a rafter, or merely leaning against a bench. Never turn it upside down for service. Doing so could crimp the brake cable housing and scuff the saddle. It's also not easy to work on a bike while doing a headstand.

Conduct this inspection when your local bike shop is open so you can hustle down for replacement parts. Always take the faulty item with you to get an exact match.

Okay, get out your fine-tooth comb and let's go. If you find a problem, consult the appropriate section of this book for the exact repair procedure.

Frame

Inspect each tube intersection. Are there fractures in the paint that indicate cracks in the lugs or welds? Owners of aluminum or carbon-fiber frames should look for a discolored ring near a joint, which indicates glue failure. If you have any doubt about your frame's integrity, consult a pro mechanic.

How's the frame's finish? It's probably too late for repainting

—the normal spring waiting list at most frame shops is eight to ten weeks—but you can stop rust from spreading. Sand any spots to bare metal with 400- or 500-grit sandpaper, then dab on primer with a small brush. This will protect the frame until you can have it repainted. If you're self-conscious with these spots, check the local toy store for model enamel close to your color. With a little mixing you can even match faded paint.

Wax the frame with Bike Elixir, Dave Moulton's Frame Wax, or an auto paste wax. Use a spray furniture polish on Imron finishes.

Wheels

Inspect the hubs for cracks or elongated spoke holes. Do the same for the rims. Look for fractures, bulges, and sidewall damage that will impair braking. Make sure no spokes are loose, bent, or broken. Any problems so far? If there are, get thee to the bike shop. A wheel failure can cause a nasty spill.

Spin each wheel and watch the rim pass the brake pads. If you see more than slight wobbling and/or hopping, it needs attention. (Don't be fooled by watching the tire, which may appear to wobble due to manufacturing irregularities.)

Grab each wheel at the rim and wiggle it sideways. Clunking or looseness means the hub needs adjustment. Remove the wheels and turn the axles with your fingers. Roughness means the axle cones are too tight or the bearings are dry. Riding the bike with any of these hub problems can cause damage that's much costlier than simple hub adjustment or repacking.

Tires

Inflate both tires to the pressure listed on the sidewall. Inspect every square millimeter of tread for cuts and embedded debris. This is a good daily habit. You can often prevent a blow-out by finding a thorn, stone, or piece of glass before it works through to the tube. Also, check tread wear. This isn't easy on new-wave bald tires, where the only tell-tale sign is the width of the section that contacts the road. As a tire wears, this section becomes wider and thinner, which increases the chances of a puncture. If you see fabriclike casing material through the tread, immediately replace the tire. Bulges in the sidewall or tears along the bead line (just above the rim) also are grounds for replacement.

If you ride tubular tires, make sure the glue still grips tightly. Reglue if you have any doubt or if the tire has been on for a year. Glue becomes brittle with age.

Brakes

With the wheels still out, inspect the brake pads. Replace them if they're worn more than a third of the way to the shoe. Otherwise, pick out any embedded material and scuff them with sandpaper to remove heat glazing.

Make sure each caliper's mounting bolt is tight.

Replace the lever hoods if they're torn, cracked, or fused to the lever body. Hoods come in various sizes, so get the ones made for your levers. Also buy new handlebar tape. With fresh hoods and tape your bike will look new.

After this step, replace each wheel and adjust the quick-release tight enough so the handle imprints your palm. Firmly tighten the axle nuts, if that's what you have.

Derailleurs

Shift through the gears to make sure the derailleurs are in adjustment. This is a good time to replace the cables and housing, especially if you have an index system that's at least a year old. Put a film of bike grease or high-viscosity oil on the cables to prevent rust. Use extra on the end buttons and the sections that pass through cable guides or housing.

Clean both derailleurs with a rag. Squirt light oil into the derailleur pivot points and pulleys, wiping off the excess.

Crankset

Check the tightness of the chainring and crankarm bolts. Check the bottom bracket adjustment by grasping the crankarms and wiggling them side to side. There should be no play.

Unship the chain and see if the crank rotates freely. Then look for warped chainrings and damaged teeth by turning the crank and sighting along the front derailleur cage from above. Wobbling chainrings can be trued.

Pedals

Check the toe clips for cracks and loose bolts. Replace the straps if they look frail or if the buckle has worn into the leather or nylon. Always save old toe straps—they're handy in many ways.

Wiggle the pedals and hope you don't feel looseness. Spin them and hope they turn freely. To be certain the adjustment is correct, remove each pedal and turn its axle with your finger. It should rotate smoothly. Pedals can be adjusted or repacked, as necessary.

Chain

Count 24 links and measure from the first pin to the last (center to center). If the distance is 12⅛ inches or more, replace the chain. Even though it may ride fine, a stretched chain causes excessive wear to the relatively expensive chainrings and freewheel. A new chain measures 12 inches between the same pins.

Whenever you replace the chain, take a test ride to check for skipping. Push hard in each freewheel cog, staying seated in case what you're looking for actually happens. Badly worn cogs won't mate with a new chain, so replace the ones that skip. If you see thin, hooked teeth on almost every cog, use this opportunity to buy a new freewheel with cog sizes better suited to your needs.

If your chain is still usable, wipe off surface grime with a rag and apply a chain lubricant. Use a small screwdriver to remove the sludge from between freewheel cogs.

Headset

With the wheels on the ground, squeeze the front brake and rock the bike back and forth. A loose headset will become apparent. If it seems okay, check for tightness by slightly elevating the front wheel and letting the handlebar turn from one extreme to the other. If it sticks in either direction, the headset is tight and needs adjustment or repacking. If the front wheel tends to lock straight ahead, the headset may have to be replaced.

Here's another check: Pick up the bike, place your ear to the saddle, and turn the handlebar. Excessive rumbling means the bearings are dirty or dry. Time for repacking.

Seatpost and Handlebar

Mark the height of your seatpost and handlebar stem with masking tape. Loosen the binder bolt and pull out the saddle/seatpost. Unscrew the stem's expander bolt three or four turns, free it with a rap from a wood or rubber mallet, and pull out the stem/handlebar. Liberally coat the stem and post with bike grease and reinstall. Tighten both until the wrench imprints your palm. This procedure will prevent the alloy parts from becoming stuck in the steel tubes. Skip this step if your frame and fork are aluminum or carbon-fiber.

Here's hoping you didn't find too much wrong. But even if repairs postpone your first ride for a day or two, it's better to be inconvenienced now than on a lonely road far from home. Even more important, a well-maintained bike is a safe bike. Don't risk a crash by riding faulty equipment.

26 EMERGENCY REPAIR KIT

A bike mechanic once rode across the country with only a pair of Vise-Grips in his tool kit. Few riders have the skill to make do with such survival gear, so here are two lists of items to help deal with on-road breakdowns. As opposed to those listed in chapter 1, weight and bulk are important considerations.

Mini-Kit

You should carry a primary tool kit on any ride that takes you farther than you'd care to return on foot. In other words, consider this kit an essential bicycle component. It stresses efficiency, low weight, and minimal bulk. There are no extraneous items.

Frame pump. It should fit snugly along the seat tube or the top tube (if the frame has a head tube pump peg). Clamp-on pump brackets are fine, too. Make sure the pump head fits the valves on your tubes.

Spare tube. Buy the correct size and valve. Dust it with talcum powder and wrap it in a plastic bag. Then wrap the bag with nylon-reinforced strapping tape to protect the tube

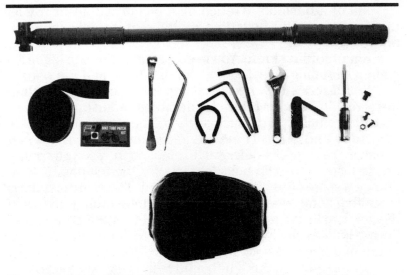

Photograph 8-1. A mini-kit for emergency repairs should include, top, a frame pump; from left to right, a spare tube, a patch kit, tire levers, a spoke wrench, Allen keys, a 4-inch adjustable wrench, a folding knife, a screwdriver, bolts and other small items; and bottom, a saddle pouch.

from chafing. This tape can also be used to make an emergency tire "boot."

Patch kit. Include a small tube of glue, four patches of various sizes, and a tire boot (1×1-inch piece of old tire casing). The boot is necessary to save a severely cut tire, a problem that's more common since the advent of high-pressure clinchers with thin casings. Wrap the patch kit in masking tape to hold it together.

Tire levers. It's nearly impossible to remove a high-pressure clincher without these. Save some weight by choosing plastic instead of steel or aluminum. Although tire levers are normally sold in sets of three, you can always get by with two.

Spoke wrench. Carry the size that fits your spoke nipples— Japanese, European, or DT. Park makes precision spoke wrenches in these sizes.

Allen keys. Carry one for each hex bolt size on the bike. This means 4, 5, 6, and sometimes 7 mm.

Small adjustable wrench. A 4-incher will fit nearly all the small nuts and bolts that might require adjustment in midvoyage.

Small folding knife. You need a single, 1¾-inch blade for cutting strapping tape, loose handlebar tape, and tire boots.

Small screwdriver(s). A ⅛-inch-blade and/or small Phillips screwdriver is necessary for derailleur adjustment screws and other small fittings, such as the computer mount.

Odds and ends. These are items you'll find useful in a pinch: a Presta-to-Schrader valve adapter (in case your pump breaks), spare toe clip bolts, change for the telephone, food money, a spare house key, and an ID card. The spare change is for calling home when all else fails. The food money gives you the freedom to extend a 60-mile ride to 100 without "bonking." Such goodies usually can be stowed in a 35mm film canister, but remember to restock it after use.

Saddle pouch. Buy a nifty under-the-seat bag to carry all this. If you own more than one bike, the bag can easily be transferred. If tire sizes are different, be sure to put in the correct spare tube.

Maxi-Kit

On multiday excursions, these items should be added to the basic kit. Unfortunately, there isn't a pro bike shop in every town on earth, so the stuff in this kit is intended to bail you out of almost any mechanical difficulty that can occur.

Folding tire and extra tube. Those of you who have asked for a 700C tire or Presta-valve tube at the hardware store in Podunk, USA, will appreciate the need to carry these items on an extended tour. Folding tires with Kevlar beads are available in virtually all sizes, including mountain bike dimensions.

Freewheel remover and Pocket Vise. Carry the appropriate remover for your freewheel and a Pocket Vise to hold the tool as you apply torque with your handlebar stem or a metal signpost. Those with a Shimano Freehub will have to carry two chainwhips in order to remove the cogs. Freewheel removal is necessary for spoke replacement on the right side of the hub.

Spare spokes. Carry nine spokes (ten if you have a 40-spoke rear wheel) to replace the ones that get mangled if the chain

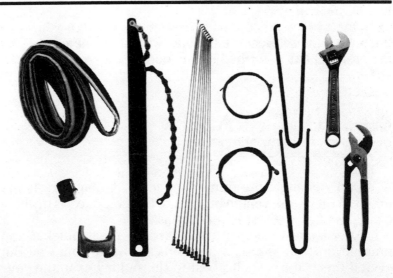

Photograph 8-2. A maxi-kit for emergency repairs should include the items in the mini-kit plus, from left to right, a folding tire, a freewheel remover, a Pocket Vise, a chainwhip, spokes, cables, adjustable cup tools, a 6-inch adjustable wrench, and pliers.

shifts into them. Make sure they are the right size. Keep spare spokes inside the frame pump, or tape them to the bike's left chainstay.

Spare cables. Properly maintained cables shouldn't break, but when they do, nothing will work in their place. Carry a rear brake cable and a rear derailleur cable (with the unneeded head removed if you buy the universal type). If a front cable breaks, install the replacement and coil the excess until you can trim it.

Adjustable cup tools. Park makes a lightweight universal pin tool and lockring tool. These are indispensable for adjusting a loose bottom bracket that would otherwise grind the crank innards into useless pulp as you pedal toward the next bike shop.

Adjustable wrench. The 6-inch size is handy for removing pedals and straightening chainrings.

Lubricants. Take a small tube of grease for sticky cables.

Pliers. A small pair of Channellock-type will do what the other tools won't.

Hand cleaner. Store a tube of this and some paper towels in a plastic bag.

One final word of advice: Never carry a tool you don't know how to use. Become familiar with all of them by doing the basic repairs described in this book.

▪27 POST-CRASH INSPECTION

Oddly enough, the primary concern of many crash victims isn't their own welfare but that of their bicycle. "Is my bike okay?" is often the first thing they ask.

After a crash, you can usually rotate the handlebar and brake levers to their proper positions and be on your way. But even if this is the case, it's best to thoroughly examine your bike once you return home so you don't have another accident due to a weakened part. Here's what to do for road and mountain bikes.

Frame and Fork

Frame. In a frontal impact, the down and top tubes take much of the force. Inspect the area where these tubes join the head tube for wrinkles and cracks in the paint that could indicate metal damage. The chainstays and seatstays sometimes bend, too. To check for this, sight down each one. Then inspect the frame for dents. Sometimes the handlebar can swing around and strike the top tube hard enough to damage it.

Small "thumbprint" dents, minor stay bends, and slight main tube bends can be repaired by a qualified mechanic. Extreme damage may require replacing a tube or even discarding the frame. In general, the best shops for such work are those that use an alignment table or build frames.

Fork. Looking from the side, an imaginary straight line through the head tube should bisect the center of the fork's top section. A straightedge can help gauge this.

The fork can also bend at the steerer (the threaded portion of the fork inside the head tube). When the blades appear unharmed but the fork is out of alignment, you should remove it and inspect the steerer.

Another check is to remove and reinstall an undamaged front wheel several times to see if the rim centers between the fork blades. If not, the blades were probably pushed to one side and must be straightened.

Have a qualified mechanic repair your fork using a jig and aligning lever. Sideways bends are easiest to fix. Forward and backward bends on high-quality forks can often be repaired, but when the blades are severely wrinkled or when the blades and steerer are bent, the fork must be replaced.

Wheels

Rims and spokes. Spin the wheels and look for lateral or vertical rim movement. Truing can correct some of this, but large wobbles or hops may require replacing the rim and spokes. (It's not worth replacing these parts on an inexpensive wheel. Instead, purchase a new one.) Locate loose spokes by wiggling each one. In a violent crash, they can pull out of the hub flange. Tighten or replace them as necessary and true the wheel.

Feel for defects in the rim sidewall by holding your fingers against it as it spins, or sight along the brake pads. Bulges can sometimes be repaired by bending with pliers and sanding.

Other parts. If wheel damage is apparent, inspect the hub flanges for cracks and bends. Such problems usually require replacing the wheel.

In addition, remove the wheel and check for a bent axle by turning it with your fingers. Replace if necessary. If the tire is flat, check the sidewalls and tread for cuts.

Other Components

Handlebar and stem. Look for scratches that may indicate these parts have been damaged. Sight across the flat portion of the handlebar (near the stem) to see if it's straight. Then view the bar from the front to see if one side is bent. If so, replace the bar. Apply new handlebar tape if necessary, and rotate the bar and stem to their correct positions after loosening the binder bolts with an Allen wrench.

Brakes. A front caliper arm can bend in a crash when it strikes the down tube. Use large pliers or an adjustable wrench to straighten it. Replace brake cable housing that is cracked or kinked. Compare the left and right brake and shift levers to see if they moved or are bent. Loosen the clamps on handlebar-mounted controls and rotate them into position. Levers with small bends can be straightened with pliers. Replace scuffed or torn brake hoods.

A rare problem is a cantilever boss fracture. This can be fixed by brazing or screwing a new boss to the frame.

Derailleurs. When a bike falls over, it can land on the rear derailleur, bending it (or the hanger) toward the spokes. One sign of possible damage is a scratched derailleur body. Also, look at your bike from behind. The derailleur cage should be parallel to the freewheel cogs. A bent derailleur should be aligned at a shop that has the proper tools to check it and the gear hanger.

Pedals and cranks. Carefully ride the bike to check for a bent pedal or crankarm. If there's damage, you'll feel it on each pedal stroke. To pinpoint the problem, install a good pedal and ride some more. If pedaling is still uncomfortable, the crankarm is bent. Bent crankarms can often be straightened by a mechanic, but damaged pedals should be replaced.

Spin the crankset to see if the chainrings are true. These can usually be straightened by gentle prying with an adjustable wrench.

Seat. Saddles are often scuffed in a crash, but such damage usually isn't serious. (Try using a Lycra seat cover to hide the abrasion.) Check under the saddle for bent or cracked rails, and replace it if such damage exists.

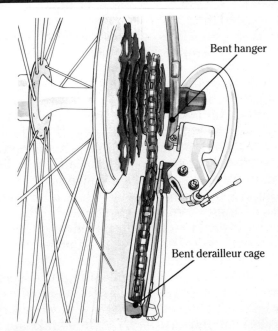

Illustration 8-1. A bent derailleur and/or hanger will cause faulty shifting.

28 BREAKING IN A NEW BIKE

"I bought a lemon!"

This thought may cross your mind a few weeks after wheeling your newfound love out of the bike shop.

Most shop managers can tell stories of customers angrily returning their bikes, complaining of loose cranks, wobbly wheels, and derailleurs that no longer index. It's a familiar test of diplomacy to patiently explain that these problems aren't fatal flaws in the merchandise, just part of breaking in a new bike. This is why most shops offer a free tune-up 30 days after purchase. Take advantage of it, then use this book to take care of future maintenance.

Why 30 days? Because within this time the cables on a new bike can stretch enough to hamper braking and disrupt index shifting, and the spokes will often seat themselves fully, causing the once perfectly true wheels to wobble. Once readjusted after this break-in period, cables and wheels should be fine for a long time.

The 30-day inspection also lets the mechanic double-check the tightness of bolts and nuts that tend to loosen during the initial miles. This is particularly true of the bolts that hold the crankarms to the bottom bracket axle. If you ignore these bolts for long, you might never be able to sufficiently tighten the crankarms. At worst, a crank can fall off while riding, causing a crash or at least a lot of inconvenience.

In addition to these problems, you may notice others after a few weeks of riding. Some you can remedy; others that may require a professional touch could include the following.

Loose bearings. Bearings in the bottom bracket, headset, and hubs are properly adjusted when they're free of side play but turn smoothly. The catch is that bearings can feel perfectly adjusted when installed, yet settle in enough to develop play after a few rides. To detect this, wiggle your wheels sideways, rock your bike back and forth with the front brake applied, and try to wiggle the bottom bracket while grasping both crankarms. (A loose bottom bracket can also result from cups that weren't tightened properly when installed. Side play can quickly damage the component's races and should be corrected immediately.)

Stiff chain link. A mechanic installing a bicycle chain will routinely ensure that the joining link has enough play to bend smoothly. But sometimes chains come from the factory with other tight links. If your feet occasionally skip forward slightly when pedaling, suspect a stiff link. To check, get off and shift into the smallest chainring/cog to minimize derailleur spring tension. While backpedaling slowly, watch each link as it curves around the derailleur's lower pulley. If you spot one that doesn't straighten as readily as the rest, loosen it by flexing the link from side to side with your hands.

Brake squeal. Unless your shop road tests each bike it sells, your brakes might shudder or squeal even if they were quiet on the test stand. Correcting this common malady involves angling each brake pad so the front end contacts the rim first. With some brakes, this "toe-in" adjustment simply requires loosening the brake shoes and retightening them in the proper position. With other brakes, the caliper arms must be bent slightly.

Loose or creaking handlebar, stem, and seat. Obviously, if the handlebar slips in the stem, the stem rotates in the steerer tube, or the saddle slips, these parts should be tightened. Less apparent is the solution to creaking noises coming from the bar, stem, or seatpost. These usually arise when pulling on the bar while climbing or sprinting, or when pedaling hard in the saddle. A light coating of grease on the stem and seatpost where they insert into the frame and where the stem clamps the handlebar will usually eliminate such bothersome noise.

Gearing changes. If you ride in hilly terrain you might desire lower gearing, particularly if your new bike is set up for racing and your legs and lungs are not. Conversely, a flatlander will find little use for wide-range touring gears and might want the greater efficiency of close-spaced ratios. A gearing swap can sometimes be negotiated before the bike leaves the showroom, but if you've ridden it for a few weeks and want to change freewheels or chainrings, consider the old parts as spares. An increasingly common drivetrain switch is from round to nonround chainrings, or vice versa. Unless you know from experience that you don't like the chainring shape on your new bike, give it a try. You might come to prefer round or elliptical rings, or, commonly, not even notice a difference.

Rotating toe straps. If you use toe straps, it's annoying to pull them tight only to have the whole strap rotate in the pedal. This is a problem with thin leather or nylon straps that don't fit snugly in the pedal slots. To prevent this, some riders put a twist in their straps between the slots (under the pedal). Others secure them to the pedal cages with plastic ties.

Underinflated tires. Inner tubes are porous enough to slowly lose air. The higher the initial pressure, the faster this happens. Thus, narrow road tires need pumping more often than wide mountain bike tires. To prevent pinch flats and minimize rolling resistance, learn how your tires feel at proper pressure when depressed by your thumb. Then check them before every ride.

■29■ PRE-EVENT CHECKLIST

There's an old maxim in bicycle racing that says, "To win, you have to finish." Fact is, this bit of wisdom applies to all cycling events, from informal group rides to centuries. You may be in the best possible condition, but it won't matter if your bike breaks.

The secret to making sure it doesn't is to conduct a thorough hour-long inspection two days before every important event. This allows you time to test any adjustments.

What follows is a detailed inspection procedure arranged according to major areas of the bicycle. You'll need most of the tools described in chapter 1.

Drivetrain

Bottom bracket bearings. Shift to the small chainring and lift the chain onto the bottom bracket with your finger. Spin the crank. It should turn freely. Wiggle the crankarms laterally to check for bearing play. If there is any roughness or looseness, use a lockring spanner and pin tool to adjust the bearings. (On most cranksets you can do this without removing the crankarms.) Even if the bottom bracket feels okay, try tightening the lockring.

Crankarm bolts. Unscrew the crankarm dust caps and

tighten the mounting bolts or nuts with a socket wrench. Grease the threads and reinstall the caps.

Chainring bolts. Tighten these with a 5mm Allen wrench. (You may need to hold the nuts on the back of the rings with your finger or a chainring bolt tool.)

Pedals. Tighten each one to the crankarm with a 15mm wrench.

Toe clips and straps. Check clips for cracks and straps for grooves that could cause slipping. Replace if necessary. Tighten the mounting hardware with a screwdriver and wrench.

Chain. Backpedal with the chain on the smallest freewheel cog. If there are any stiff links, you'll see them snag the rear derailleur pulleys. To remedy this, grasp the chain on either side of the stiff link and work it until it loosens. If there are more than two stiff links, replace the chain.

Next, measure the chain with a ruler. Start on the center of any pin and look at the 12-inch mark. If that pin is ⅛ inch or more past the mark, the chain has stretched and should be replaced.

Apply spray lube and go for a short ride. Pedal hard in each gear to test for skipping. This commonly occurs after replacing the chain and indicates worn teeth on the freewheel cogs. To correct this, replace the freewheel.

Gear cables. Check at the levers, under the bottom bracket, and near the derailleur anchor bolts for rusting and fraying. Replace if necessary. If shifting is sluggish, grease the cables where they pass through the housing.

Rear derailleur. Shift to make sure there is no hesitation when going to the largest or smallest cog. If shifting is sluggish or if the chain derails, adjust the limit screws. (These are sometimes marked L for low gear and H for high gear.)

To fine-tune an index system, use the adjustment barrel located where the cable enters the derailleur. Turning the barrel counterclockwise quickens shifting to larger cogs, while turning it clockwise improves shifting to smaller ones. Adjust it a half turn at a time, then check performance. (For more information, see chapter 13.)

Front derailleur. Shift forcefully, making sure the chain doesn't fall off and the cage doesn't hit the crankarm. If either happens, adjust the limit screws.

Derailleur bolts. Gently tighten the bolts that secure the derailleurs, pulleys, front derailleur cage, and cables.

Wheels

Hub bearings. Remove both wheels. Grasp the axle lock-nuts and try unscrewing them with your fingers. If they loosen, use cone wrenches to tighten them against the cones. (On rear wheels this requires removing the freewheel.) Turn the axle to check for resistance. Loosen the cone adjustment if necessary. Check bearing play by trying to move the axle up and down. A little play is permissible if it disappears when the wheel is clamped in the frame. Once the wheels are installed, recheck the play by trying to move the rim laterally. If there is movement, remove the wheel and tighten the cone adjustment.

Spokes. Wiggle each one. Tighten as necessary, and true the wheels with a spoke wrench.

Tires. They should have ample tread (no bare patches) and no large cuts. Also, check the sidewalls for cracks. If problems exist, replace the tires. Another test is to inflate the tires and spin them to make sure there are no flat or high spots. If the tires aren't round, let the air out and reinflate. If the problem persists, buy new tires.

Brakes

Mounting bolts. Gently tighten the two brake mounting nuts located behind the fork crown and in front of the rear brake bridge. Use a 5mm Allen wrench or a 10mm open-end wrench. Tighten cantilever brakes with a 5 or 6mm Allen wrench.

Lubrication. Spray some lube on the pivots and brake springs. (Don't get any on the brake pads or tires.)

Pads. If they've worn past their grooves, replace them. Be sure they don't touch the tire or go under the rim when the brakes are applied. Tighten their mounting nuts or bolts.

Cables. Inspect these for fraying inside the levers. Check for resistance that might indicate a bad cable. Lubricate or replace as necessary.

Front End

Headset bearings. Check these by turning the handlebar with the front wheel off the ground. If the fork turns roughly, loosen the top nut and the adjusting cone underneath. Then tighten the nut and cone against each other with a pair of headset wrenches, or one headset wrench and large locking pliers.

With both wheels on the ground, rock the bike back and forth while applying the front brake. A clunking noise indicates bearing play. Another way to check for this is to lift the front wheel several inches off the ground and drop it, listening for a rattling noise. Tighten the bearing adjustment if necessary.

Even if your headset passes these tests, make sure the nut and cone are tight against each other.

Handlebar and stem. Check for stem tightness by lightly turning the handlebar with the front wheel between your knees. Press down on the ends of the bar to see if it rotates. Use a 5 or 6mm Allen wrench to tighten the stem expander bolt or the handlebar binder bolt as necessary.

Levers. Check the tightness of brake and mountain bike shift levers by trying to twist them on the handlebar. To tighten drop bar brake levers, use a 4 or 5mm Allen wrench or an 8mm socket inside the lever. Mountain bike controls are tightened with a 4, 5, or 6mm Allen wrench or an 8mm open-end wrench.

Seat

Saddle and seatpost. Tighten the seat clamp (under the saddle) with a 13mm open-end wrench or a 6mm Allen wrench. Try twisting the saddle and seatpost in the frame. If it turns, tighten the seatpost binder bolt with a 5mm Allen wrench. On mountain bikes, tighten the quick-release lever.

Accessories

Water bottle cages. Inspect them for cracks and replace if necessary. Gently tighten the mounting bolts.

Tire repair kit. Examine your spare tube and repair kit. Make sure the glue hasn't dried. Include a piece of sailcloth or denim. This can be temporarily placed inside the tire to "boot" large slits. Inflate a tire to check the operation of your frame pump.

CREDITS

The information in this book is drawn from these and other articles in *Bicycling* magazine.

"Home Shop Tools" Don Cuerdon, "Home Shop Tools," January/February 1987.

"Weekly Maintenance" Don Cuerdon, "Weekly Maintenance," July 1987.

"Lightning Lube" Don Cuerdon, "Lightning Lube," August 1988.

"Eliminating Ticks and Rattles" Don Cuerdon, "Ticks, Squeaks and Ratttles," September 1987.

"Wash and Wax" Jim Langley, "Wash and Wax," April 1989.

"Clincher Tire Repair" Don Cuerdon, "Clincher Tire Repair," April 1988.

"Pump Repair" Jim Langley, "Air to Spare," January/February 1989.

"Wheel Truing" Jim Langley, "The Whole Truth . . . ," January/February 1990.

"Spoke Replacement" Don Cuerdon, "Twaang!" May 1988.

"Easy Rim Replacement" Jim Langley, "Rim Replacement," June 1989.

"Servicing Caliper Brakes" Don Cuerdon, "Caliper Brakes," May 1987.

"Cantilevers and U-Brakes" Jim Langley, "Stop Watch," December 1989.

"Installing and Adjusting an Index Shifting System" Jim Langley, "Index Shifting Systems," March 1989.

"Gear System Tune-Up" Don Cuerdon, "Gear System Tune-Up," June 1988.

"Chain Care" Jim Langley, "Chain Reactions," September 1989.

"Freewheel Cog Replacement" Don Cuerdon, "Freewheel Cog Replacement," December 1987.

"Crankset Overhaul" Don Cuerdon, "Crankset Overhaul," July 1988.

"Hub Overhaul" Don Cuerdon, "Hub Overhaul," January/February 1988.

"Headset Overhaul" Fred Zahradnik, "Headset Overhaul," September 1988.

"Pedal Overhaul" "Pedals," July 1986.

"Care and Cleaning" Don Cuerdon and Gary Fisher, "The Care and Cleaning of an ATB," May 1987.

"Frame Paint Touch-Up" Don Cuerdon, "Frame Touch-Up," October/November 1987.

"Weatherproofing" Jim Chapman, "Weatherproofing," December 1988.

"Personal Adjustments" Jim Langley, "Frontal Adjustments," May 1989.

"Spring Tune-Up" Don Cuerdon, "Your Bike," May 1987.

"Emergency Repair Kit" Don Cuerdon, "Emergency Repair Kit," April 1987.

"Post-Crash Inspection" Jim Langley, "Crash Course," August 1989.

"Breaking In a New Bike" Jim Langley, "Breaking In a New Bike," March 1989.

"Pre-Event Checklist" Jim Langley, "Pre-Event Checkup," July 1989.

Photographs and Illustrations

John P. Hamel: photo 1-1; Joe Griffin: photos 8-1, 8-2.

Illustrations by Sally Onopa.

Rodale Press, Inc., publishes BICYCLING, America's leading cycling magazine.
For information on how to order your subscription,
write to BICYCLING, Emmaus, PA 18098.